4/94   6

César Vallejo was born in Santiago de Chuco, Peru, in 1892. He studied law and literature in Trujillo and in 1917 moved to Lima. In 1921 he spent three months in prison where he wrote many of the poems in *Trilce*. In 1923 he left for Paris, where he co-founded a cell of the Peruvian Communist Party. From Paris, he traveled to Russia and to Spain, during the Spanish Civil War. He died in Paris, in absolute poverty, devastated by the fall of the Spanish Republic, in 1938. Besides a novel, a drama, and several journalistic and political writings, Vallejo left five books of poetry. Of these only *The Black Heralds* (*Los heraldos negros*, 1918) and *Trilce* (1922) were published during Vallejo's lifetime. *Payroll of Bones* (*Nómima de huesos* 1923–1936), *Sermon on Barbarism* (*Sermón de la barbarie* 1936–1938) and *Spain, Take This Cup from Me* (*España, aparta de mí este cáliz* 1937–1938) were published posthumously as *Poemas Humanos* (*Human Poems*).

Trilce was published in the same year as *The Waste Land* and is, like the Eliot poem, a masterpiece of early modernism, a ground–breaking work which had an indelible effect on all subsequent poetry in its language. The book contains seventy-seven poems that are considered Vallejo's most complex and radical work.

Clayton Eshleman is one of America's most distinguished poets, translators, and editors. Over the past twenty–five years, Black Sparrow Press has brought out ten collections of his poetry. His 1978 cotranslation of César Vallejo's *Complete Posthumous Poetry* received the 1979 National Book Award. He has also cotranslated all of Aimé Césaire's poetry, as well as significant sections of Antonin Artaud, Micheal Deguy, Pablo Neruda, Bernard Bador, and Vladimir Holan. He has edited two seminal literary magazines: *Caterpillar* (1967–1974) and *Sulfur* (1981 to present). He is Professor of English at Eastern Michigan University.

Américo Ferrari is Professor of Translation Methodology at the Geneva University in Switzerland and the editor of the *Obra poética de César Vallejo*, published by the Colección Archivos.

Julio Ortega is a professor in the Hispanic Studies Department at Brown University and the editor of the critical edition of *Trilce* published by Editorial Cátedra.

D1566237

CÉSAR VALLEJO

TRILCE

Translated by Clayton Eshleman

Spanish text established by Julio Ortega
Introduction by Américo Ferrari

Marsilio Publishers
New York, New York

Earlier drafts of many of these poems appeared in the following magazines: *Anteus, Denver Quarterly, Grand Street, Mandorla, Mid–American Review, o•blēk, Review,* and *Sulfur.* Poem XXXVIII appeared as *Ta'wil Broadside #7.* · The translator gratefully acknowledges a Research Fellowship (1988-1990) from Eastern Michigan University, travel support from the World College at Eastern Michigan University, and a generous grant from the Wheatland Foundation.

Table of Contents

INTRODUCTION

Américo Ferrari

This year, 1992, marks the one hundredth anniversary of César Vallejo's birth. Official homages and university colloquia will do their part to promulgate his name, his biography, and certain aspects of his work (which in some cases will reveal more about the ideologies of Vallejo's critics than about the arcana of Vallejo's poetry). Though the intention underlying the publication of any great poet's work is always praiseworthy, the excess of publicity surrounding this poet's name has the disadvantage of clouding over his work's obscure clarity: easy paths are laid out for readers in search of facts or information, and it is often forgotten that the speech of any truly poetic work encloses an unspeakable where, perhaps, the nucleus of the living relation between the poem and the world resides. Neither the reader, nor the critic, nor the translator, nor even the poet himself nor his very poem can declare what this secret place is because it forms part of the very form that structures the poetic expression. However, the reality of this secret place can show itself, as Ludwig Wittgenstein argues with respect to all representations of reality mediated by a system of signs, and it becomes even more palpable when it is the reality of a world perceived, as Vallejo himself testified, by four consciousnesses merged into one. Vallejo's poems show, more than say, their light and their shadows; they are, Rafael Gutiérrez Girardot has suggested, "sonorous gestures." That is why the poet asks that his poems be "heard as a single mass" and why he invents "a suitable alphabet": he demands that his reader become an accomplice who shoulders, with the same fears and the same hopes as the poet, the poetry's "vast and rough mass" and who longs to recognize its alphabet and to recognize himself in it. For that reason, too—it must be said in this year of public homages and commentaries—the best international homage that can be rendered is a good translation, one that incorporates the mass and the alphabet of these poems into another language, restoring them directly and without commentary to the concrete singularity of the sonorous gesture, and impelling the reader toward a double profundity: that of the Spanish text and that of its translation. This is perhaps one of the best ways, and certainly one of the most direct ways, of extending a bridge toward the meaning of this difficult poetry, and of cutting through some parts of the wide network of misconceptions in which the destiny of this body of work has been entangled for many years, a destiny its author shares with others such as Arthur Rimbaud or Antonin Artaud who, with Vallejo, have been dubbed by Clayton Eshleman "conductors of the pit."

Vallejo was ill-fated where the publication of his work was concerned. Though it did enjoy relative critical success, his first book, *Los heraldos negros,* was never reprinted during the poet's life, and the reader who failed to acquire it in 1919 had to wait thirty years before it was reissued in 1949, in the *Poesías completas* published by

Losada. *Trilce,* his second book, fell into a void, as its author tersely declared; but thanks to the intervention of "the good fairies," as
Juan Larrea called them—Gerardo Diego, José Bergamín and Larrea himself—a second edition was published in 1930, and did its
part in attracting the attention of readers of poetry to its author
who was, at that point, still ignored and already forgotten. Vallejo
died in 1938 without seeing the rest of his poetic work even partially published, except for a few poems that appeared in magazines.
After *Trilce,* then, virtually all of Vallejo's poetry is posthumous.

When the first edition of *Los heraldos negros* came out in mid-
July 1919, Vallejo had already written several of the poems that
would form *Trilce;* in the second half of that year, he probably
wrote many others, including many of those that evoke his relationship with Otilia Villanueva, which was broken off either that
very July, as Coyné conjectures, or else in May, if we are to believe
Vallejo's friend Juan Espejo Asturrizaga. Be that as it may, the years
between 1918 and 1922 are crucial in Vallejo's life and in the evolution of his poetry.

Two absences mark these years: that of the poet's mother and,
as 1919 began, that of Otilia, who seems in certain poems to be
conflated with two other absent women, Zoila Rosa Cuadra,
known as Mirtho, and another Otilia who lived in Santiago de
Chuco, Vallejo's home town. To these absences can perhaps be added the figure of another dead woman, María Rosa Sandóval, to
whom Vallejo had alluded in one of the poems of *Los heraldos
negros,* "The Eternal Dice." Vallejo's mother died in August 1918,
but it was only in the years following her death that Vallejo would
grasp the full extent and particular spirit of his orphanhood, as it is

revealed throughout *Trilce* by the relentless presence of death in the emptiness of the past. In his poems' representations of death, Vallejo also represents his native region, his Andean landscape, his home, the games he played with his brothers ("Miguel who has died..."), the ritual of meals which were the agape and holy communion of the still intact home. All of these things reveal their absence in the absence of the mother; and the absent beloveds, the absence of loves that have died, are connected with her as well. Though the Lima Otilia is the central character in the poems' sentimental and erotic evocations (often garbed in a marked transcendence and linked to Vallejo's obsessions with existence and death), the last love probably alternates, as Larrea has emphasized, with the other beloveds, or may sometimes merge with them in a dream-like vision in which several faces are compounded in a single face. For at least two of these women, the Andean beloved and the Lima beloved, the shared name of Otilia linguistically facilitates this kind of amalgamation (see poem XLII). Moreover, we can join with Coyné in thinking that the more crudely erotic poems may refer to some ephemeral sexual adventure.

It would therefore be highly imprudent to try to link these poems' vision with specific biographical anecdotes in a strict and unidimensional way, as Espejo frequently does. To complicate such connections even further, Vallejo repeatedly finds, or tries to find, the attributes of the mother in the beloved; this could already be seen in *Los heraldos negros:* "Unnail these nails from me, oh new mother of mine!" ("Nervasion of Anguish"), and it becomes apparent once more in poem XLVI of *Trilce* in which the poet gets filially up from the table where Otilia has just eaten. In *Trilce,* eroticism and the presence of the female reach their culminating point in Vallejo's work. They will reappear in only two or three of the European poems, and in a much attenuated form.

Imprisonment is the other determinative experience of the *Trilce* years. For details of the absurd allegation that Vallejo participated in certain disturbances which occurred in Santiago de Chuco on August 1, 1920, the reader may consult the works by Espejo and Coyné. After spending a two-month vacation in his home town, the poet had returned to Trujillo at the beginning of July when he suddenly decided to go back to Santiago, where the festival in honor of the town's patron saint was about to take place, and where the political situation was "highly inflammable," according to Espejo. After the events of August 1, an examining magistrate sent from Trujillo had twelve people detained for questioning, among whom were César Vallejo and two of his brothers, Víctor and Manuel. Before any formal charges were filed, the Trujillo newspaper *La Industria* published a denunciation of Vallejo, which he subsequently refuted (see his *Epistolario general*). At the end of August, Vallejo was formally charged as the intellectual instigator of the events, at which point he went into hiding at Antenor Orrego's country house in Mansiche, near Trujillo. On November 7 he was arrested in Trujillo and remained in prison there until February 26, 1921. The experience of prison was preceded, then, by the anguish of more than two months of persecution and clandestine life. More than a dozen of the poems in *Trilce* belong to this period of persecution and imprisonment; in them, hope, the anxiety of a hunted man, and the oppression of the cell's four walls alternate with evocation and memory. From prison, he writes to his friend Oscar

Imaña on February 12, 1921: "In my cell I read from time to time; from moment to moment I brood and gnaw my elbows with rage, not so much for the dishonor of it as for the material deprivation, the utterly material deprivation of my animal freedom. It is an ugly thing, Oscar. I also write now and then, and if some sweet breath of air does come to my soul, it is the light of memory. Oh, memory in prison! How it comes and falls in the heart, oiling with its melancholy the machine that is now so broken..."

"I also write now and then..." Actually, during the 112 days he spent in prison, in addition to the eight poems in *Trilce* indicated by Espejo, Vallejo also wrote the first of the short narratives that make up *Escalas.* Already, in *La Crónica* of July 20, 1921, the Peruvian writer Juan José Lora, presenting early versions of three of the poems which would appear in *Trilce,* says that Vallejo has written (in prison, we can understand from the context) a book of prose and another of poetry, the latter entitled *Escalas.* This, as far as we know, is the first time that the title *Escalas,* under which Vallejo would publish a collection of prose texts in 1923, is mentioned. Whether Vallejo had spoken to Lora of a prose work titled *Escalas* and a still untitled book of poetry and his friend had confused the two, or the poet had at first thought of using *Escalas* as the title of what would later become *Trilce,* the composition of the two books partially overlaps, and the two are closely related, not only because of the shared themes, figures and obsessions that dominate them— as Coyné, Neale-Silva and Paoli have observed—but also in the texture of their writing: the prose of *Escalas* has many features in common with the poetic expression of *Trilce,* with its tensions, its ruptures, and its silences. In addition, three prose poems in *Trilce*

(LXIV, LXX and LXXV) connect it not only to *Escalas* but also to the first of the Paris poems.

The evolution of Vallejo's poetic writing between 1918 and 1922, together with the poet's painful life experiences during those years, has a determinative importance for the meaning and the design of *Trilce*. The forms, the difficult writing that was already gestating in certain of the poems of *Los heraldos negros*, require the reader's ceaseless collaboration. Almost every link to symbolism and modernism is broken. It should not surprise us, therefore, that in the literary environment of the Lima of those years, when even a good-mannered modernism was still barely acceptable, the only criticism the book received, in general, was silence. There is very little to say about its reception. There was no reception. Even Mariátegui devotes very few lines to it in the passages on Vallejo in his *Siete ensayos*, which are almost entirely dedicated to *Los heraldos negros*. "The book has fallen into a total void," the poet stated. More or less the same thing had happened to José Maria Eguren's *Simbólicas* in 1911.

Here, it might be worthwhile to look again at two passages from the *Epistolario general*, already abundantly cited by critics, which can amply attest to the attitude that the Vallejo of those years had regarding poetic creation:

The book has fallen into a total void. I am responsible for the book. I assume complete responsibility for its aesthetics. Today, perhaps more than ever, I sense an until now unknown and sacred obligation gravitating over me as a man and as an artist: to be free! If I am not free today, I never will be. I feel the arch of my forehead swell with its most imperious curve of heroism. I give myself over to the freest form that I can, and this is my greatest artistic harvest. God alone knows the degree to which my freedom is certain and true! God knows how much I have suffered to keep this rhythm from overrunning that freedom and spilling into license! God knows over what hair-raising edges I have peered, brimming with fear that everything in the depths would die so that my poor soul might live!

I want to be free, no matter what sacrifices I must make. In being free, I sometimes feel surrounded by the most frightening ridicule, like a child who mistakenly lifts his spoon up to his nose.

There is perhaps no better explanation than Vallejo's own for *Trilce,* and for the void into which it fell. Critics had no means of grasping it, no norms or standards by which to judge this writing and to measure this freedom. Even the few Peruvian critics who were more or less closely following the movement of the avant-gardes in Europe and in America were at a loss: in 1922, even the avant-garde had its handles, its norms and its measures. *Trilce* astonished a poet as wide-ranging as Emilio Adolfo Westphalen, who was brought up on contemporary poetry. In *Otra imagen deleznable* (1980), Westphalen writes of his first reading of the book in the 1930s: "...A very surprising reading of *Trilce*... Nothing that I know of in avant-garde poetry had prepared me for the encounter with this force of nature."

INTRODUCTION

One of the Paris poems, "Discovery of Life," represents an experience of life in which pleasure comes from the unheard-of nature of an emotion and the poet lives as if he had never lived before. In the same way, the language of *Trilce* expresses an unheard-of emotion and the poet discovers it as he creates it, as if there had never been writing before. All of this can serve to explain the indifference with which Vallejo saw his book fall into the void of the literary circles of Lima: "It neither surprised me nor affected me," the poet's wife says he declared to her. In any case he had already decided to sever his ties and travel to Europe, a decision he carried out in June 1923, after the publication of *Escalas*.

The world of *Trilce* is a strange world, full of boundaries and spikes, where every liberating impulse is frustrated between the four walls of the cell, in the prisons of obsessive memory, in the labyrinths of sensation, in the pure immediacy of existence where reality is fragmented, absurd, unintelligible: "However I imagine my life / or imagine not having yet been born, / I will not succeed in freeing myself" (XXXIII). Man, with his hopes and the dolorous grandeur that vibrates in the posthumous poems, is almost totally absent in *Trilce*: it is an empty, obscure and hostile world that fills us with the fear of the "coarse, colossal block" (LXXIII)—a world whose two poles are immediate sensation and memory, the perception of incoherent diversity and the closed space of the irremediable. The future is closed, the world of distances and far horizons, the true human world, is closed, too, and the poet feels immobilized: "I push no further," he mutters. Fear circulates through the pages of *Trilce*: fear, perhaps, of the widening abyss between the prison in which the poet struggles against himself and a human

world of openness and hope. In connection with this obscure feeling of fear, Vallejo refers, in poem XXVII, to certain "exploded
bridges," a transparent symbol of isolation and separation; in poem XLIX, the spikes of the gratings, the closed wardrobe, and the
dressing room where "there's—there Is nobody," are signs of solitude, absence, void and death.

This is why the experience of *Trilce,* imperious and fascinating
as it was, could not continue, and could not be attempted except
as a limited and unrepeatable exploration. With this book, Vallejo
conquers his freedom as a poet in the freedom of his language, but
this path of liberation is also a cul-de-sac. Following, as if in a hal-
lucination, the stifled explosions of sensation, the elemental impulse of emotions, the obsessive fixations of an abolished childhood, the language runs the risk of exhausting itself before it has
even come into being, and ends up confusing itself with the rubble
of an absurd world. At that extreme, the only choice left is silence,
pure and simple. Vallejo chose to persevere in the poetic enterprise.

* * *

There are, as Walter Benjamin says, works that are born to be
translated, that demand translation because—no matter what language they were written in—their form and their meaning emerge
out of an underlying primary and universal language that seeks to
erupt into language after language, affirming its originality in the
concrete universality of its translations. *Trilce* is one such work and
it exerts an inevitable attraction on the poet-translator. It attracts
as the abyss attracts: to translate it is to leap into the void, because

Trilce, Trilce's words, the grammar and semantics of *Trilce's* text frequently thwart the translator, as they thwart the Spanish-speaking reader, with a distance and resistance that are *almost* insurmountable. As in the physics of uncertainty, where it is impossible to determine both the position and the velocity of a particle at the same time and with the same precision, it is often almost impossible in a work like this one to determine, for each individual word, at once the vertiginous movement of the meaning and the precise, circumscribed designation of a referent. For the reader who encounters the text in Spanish, and even more for the translator who must transport them into English, *Trilce's* words can rapidly become an obsession and a nightmare. Contrary to the superficial saying, "Words are not translated, meaning is translated," the translator of this book knows that he must above all translate *words*, one by one, in order to master the scope of the meaning.

The dedication with which Clayton Eshleman (who has already given the English-speaking world one of the best translations of Vallejo's posthumous poems) has born the weight of this obsession for the paste several years is admirable. Having followed the process through our very rewarding correspondence, I am well aware of the struggle that he has carried on with this text, his long journey through the trilcic night and the patient labor of his quest through the lexical labyrinths. "I *yearn*, like Tantalus, to BE FREE of this project," Clayton wrote me as late as December 1991. Every true translation of a poetic work is, fundamentally, an attempt at translation, and in that it corresponds to the roots of the original work, particularly in Vallejo's case: his attempt in writing *Trilce* was to be free, and he explains in a letter: "God knows over what hair-raising edges I have peered"—in order to be free, so that his "poor soul might live." We have the impression that Eshleman, translating *Trilce*, has peered over those same hair-raising edges. There is in him an evident affinity with César Vallejo and others of his poetic race, "creators of profundity": and it is this affinity which truly guarantees his fidelity to the text. Among all existing translations, this is without doubt the one that touches the hidden nerve of Vallejo's work most directly, the one that best carries on —rather than reproduces—the movement and the gesture of freedom from which it was born.

TRANSLATOR'S NOTE

1922 was a banner year for international modernism. It brought us Joyce's *Ulysses*, Eliot's *The Waste Land,* Pasternak's *My Sister, Life*, e.e. cummings' *The Enormous Room*, Valery's *Le cimetière marin*, Rilke's *Duineser Elegien* (completed in 1922, then published in 1923), and of course Vallejo's *Trilce*. This medium-length work falls somewhere between Joyce's "soup pot as big as the Phoenix Park" and Eliot's "food in tins." In poem LXXI, Vallejo refers to the book as "my succulent snack of unity."

Trilce has not attracted a great deal of attention outside the Spanish-speaking world because it has not been satisfactorily translated. Over the years, a handful of American and English translators have produced English versions of its most simple-to-translate narrative poems. These translations, placed in anthologies to represent Vallejo in his "*Trilce* phase," tend to misrepresent *Trilce* as a whole, and to make Vallejo look fairly conventional. In 1973, David Smith published a version of the entire book. Unprepared for *Trilce's* carnivorous lyricism, he produced a work that is, for the wrong reasons, more obscure than Vallejo's. A barely adequate French version by Gérard de Cortanze appeared in 1983, without much resonance among French readers.

Most of what I have to say about this translation of *Trilce* is conveyed in the *Notes* that follow the translation. In a nutshell, my attempt has been

1) to respect Vallejo's text, taking no liberties whatsoever with words that can be translated directly, i.e., no attempt to improve on the text or to out-wit it,

2) to research all archaic, rare, and technical words, translating them (in contrast to guessing at them or explaining them) in such a way that the integrity of the text is not loosened up or constricted, and

3) to bring the English up to Vallejo's performance level in Spanish. This means not only creating neologisms in English to match Spanish equivalents, and finding archaic English words to match their archaic equivalents, but also occasionally inventing phrases in English that take the sound and obscurity as well as the meaning of the Spanish into consideration.

On the few occasions when I have departed from a literal, conventional translation of a word or phrase, I mention these in the *Notes*, attempting to give the reader the essential information on which my decisions were based. While referentiality passes in and out of these poems with maddening irregularity, most of the poems have an identifiable context which offers some support for the most difficult decisions.

I began to read and to translate Vallejo while I was a student at Indiana University in the late 1950s. While in Kyoto, Japan, in the early 1960s, I decided to apprentice myself to Vallejo's *Poemas humanos* (his poetry written in Europe between 1923 and 1938, and now referred to as either the posthumous poetry or the Paris poems). The fruit of this initial attempt appeared in 1968, as the *Human Poems,* published by Grove Press. Over the following years, I became dissatisfied with my work, and in the early 1970s teamed up with José Rubia Barcia, in Los Angeles, with whom I retranslated all of this work. This retranslation appeared in 1978 as *César Vallejo: The Complete Posthumous Poetry* (University of California Press). When I included fifty-five of these poems in *Conductors of the Pit: Major Works of Rimbaud, Vallejo, Cesaire, Artaud, and Holan* (Paragon House, 1988), I made further revisions. Over the years, Vallejo's poetry has become my primary aesthetic and moral source.

The European poetry is rife with translation problems, but for the most part the translator can depend upon thematic development and some referential stability. Such is not true for the most difficult poems in Trilce which, while coherent rather than arbitrary, tend to move in non-sequitur clusters, as if goaded by perceptions and arguments that are abandoned before they become clear. Poems which still resist any thorough critical discussion are placed next to the most accessible and sentimental poems Vallejo ever wrote. Which is to say that Trilce contains extremes of obscurity and simplicity which combine and fuse in the later European poems, all of which are underscored by the poet's Marxist commitment of the late 1920s. While the European poetry never becomes political in a doctrinaire sense, it is weighted with an awareness of the "other"" that in Trilce is restricted to people Vallejo personally knew—his family, his friends, and his lovers. However, there is a bravura and experimental daring to much of Trilce that Vallejo lost once he left Peru and became slowly and sadly composted into his own dying

and into the fate of Europe, especially that of Spain during the Spanish Civil War. At the same time, his suffering in Europe brought out
a dimension of compassion that is only obliquely present in *Trilce*—
where it is fixed upon his mother, and not upon what could justly be
called the human condition. In Europe, he also lost contact with the
stinging tast of Eros which drives through *Trilce* like a huge gold-
plated hearse.

* * *

Over the past three years, a number of friends and colleagues
have made useful responses to various drafts of the translation. I
want to thank especially Eliot Weinberger, George Angel, and
Américo Ferrari, and I also want to thank Walter Mignolo, Theo-
doro Maus, Esther Allen, Dennis Preston, Cecila Vicuña, and José
Rubia Barcia. I have probably talked out loud to myself more
over this period than in all the rest of my life, so I must also acknowledge and thank my wife, Caryl Eshleman, who often made
astute responses to my muttering and only occasionally asked me
to be quiet.

Up through the third draft, I found others' versions of *Trilce* useful—mainly to think against. When H.R. Hays, Reginald Gibbons,
and David Smith were translating from *Trilce,* they had no one or
hardly anyone before them to consult and argue with. As one working in this kind of darkness with Vallejo's European poetry (some of
which had been translated, much not) in the 1960s, I know how be-
wildering it can be at times to simply be alone with one's own transla-
tion-in-process.

Some indication of Julio Ortega's role in this translation must be offered. Ortega, who teaches at Brown University, is the editor of the critical edition of *Trilce* published in Madrid in 1991, and established the definitive Spanish text that appears in the present edition and that I used as the basis of my translation. In 1989, Ortega accepted my invitation to co-translate *Trilce*, and the first draft, worked out in the fall of 1989 and winter of 1990, was a shared effort. Ortega also made useful comments on the third and seventh drafts in the following year, but at this point it was becoming clear that we had serious differences in our interpretations of Vallejo. I have tried to indicate some of these in particular poem notes, and have commented in general on our disagreements when discussing the use of other scholars' speculations and research. After reading the final version of the translation in 1992, and finding that it was considerably different than the much earlier version he had last commented on, Ortega decided to withdraw his name as co-translator.

Our irreconcilable interpretations represent, on one level, the impossibility of any two people (let alone one!) reaching an all-over satisfaction with a *Trilce* translation. However, the task of trying to reconcile two minds to one translation proved an important incentive to further tune the work and this final version is, in part, the result of that effort. The irony is that buried in the archive of the book (containing more than thirty versions of some of the most difficult poems and at least fifteen versions of the rest) is a *Trilce* translational archeological dig that, were the technical means available, might very well be an important part of what the American reader should confront in this devastatingly slippery book.

While it is hard to overstate the difficulties involved in arriving at a final version of *Trilce* in English, I would not want to pass the reader on into the text itself with a feeling that it is the difficulties themselves that have triumphed in this translation. While I do not claim to have the last word on a book that will hopefully stimulate readers in many interesting interpretational directions, I am very proud of the translation and feel that it is equal to my understanding of the book. That is, when a word can be translated accurately in more than one way, I have made my final choice on the basis of not only the entire poem in question, but on what the choice may mean in terms of the book at large. In inventing English neologisms to match Spanish neologisms, I have tried for solutions that in their own way seem as inventive as Vallejo's, and that do not simply indicate the meaning of the original. At the same time, I have tried to keep my inventions in touch with the meaning, so that they do not end up being merely acrobatic. Perhaps it is not far-fetched to think of a *Trilce* translator as a kind of ring-master in a circus, with levels of sound and shades of meaning like a herd of horses whose movements and performances must be synchronized.

Clayton Eshleman
March 1992

NOTE ON THE SPANISH TEXT

This Spanish text of *Trilce* is based on the first edition, and takes into consideration editorial decisions from other recent establishments of the text. In dealing with *Trilce*, scholars face a series of complicated editorial options. The original typescript of *Trilce* no longer exists. Though two editions of the book appeared during Vallejo's lifetime, neither the first nor the second is free of problems. Thanks to Juan Espejo Asturrizaga we know that Vallejo asked one of his friends to take care of proofreading the first edition (1922). From Juan Larrea we know that Vallejo did not provide a clean copy of his book for the second Madrid edition (1930); instead, it was composed from a typed manuscript made by Gerardo Diego from Larrea's copy of the first edition; not surprisingly, it adds new typos. In his many letters to Diego, Vallejo didn't even raise the issue of typos to be corrected from the first edition.

In any event, I have had to make the following decisions:

1) There are obvious typos in the first edition that must be corrected.

2) There are many orthographical inaccuracies. How many of these Vallejo is responsible for, and how many are his proofreading

friend's oversights, or mistakes by the pressmen resetting the text by hand, is impossible to say.

3) There are other peculiarities of the first edition, such as its punctuation and spacing, that must be scrutinized.

Because most publishers of *Trilce* editions have published a copy of a circulating edition, mistakes have been perpetuated. Consequently, and in accordance with the basic common sense of textual editing, I have decided to base the text on the first edition. In establishing it, I have endeavored:

1) To correct all self-evident typos.

2) To keep all orthographical variations that seem systematic.

3) To revise these few cases in which the meaning of the poem is at odds with the word (*para* instead of *por* in XXI, for example).

4) To keep peculiarities of spacing and punctuation.

Most existing editions have preferred to grammaticalize Vallejo's deviations from standard use, but to do this is to deny the fact that *Trilce* is in every way a systematic subversion of codes, forms, and habits. In many cases, the oral voice introduces variations, mainly in the form of neologisms, that sound almost "natural" or idiomatic to vernacular Spanish.

I have taken into consideration the well-known editions of *Trilce* by Larrea and Américo Ferrari, whose Colección Archivos edition has been especially useful.

Thus besides this translation of *Trilce*, the reader of the Marsilio edition also has a newly established Spanish text.

Julio Ortega

TRILCE

Translated by Clayton Eshleman
Spanish text established by Julio Ortega

I

Quién hace tánta bulla, y ni deja
testar las islas que van quedando.

Un poco más de consideración
en cuanto será tarde, temprano,
y se aquilatará mejor
el guano, la simple calabrina tesórea
que brinda sin querer,
en el insular corazón,
salobre alcatraz, a cada hialóidea
grupada.

Un poco más de consideración,
y el mantillo líquido, seis de la tarde
DE LOS MÁS SOBERBIOS BEMOLES.

Y la península párase
por la espalda, abozaleada, impertérrita
en la línea mortal del equilibrio.

TRILCE

I *

Who's making all that racket, and not even leaving
testation to the islands beginning to appear.

A little more consideration
as it will be late, early,
and easier to assay
the guano, the simple fecapital ponk   **
a brackish gannet
toasts unintentionally,
in the insular heart, to each hyaloid
       squall.

A little more consideration,
and liquid muck, six in the evening
OF THE MOST GRANDIOSE B-FLATS.

And the peninsula raises up
from behind, muzziled, unterrified   *
on the fatal balance line.

* See the *Notes* that follow the translation
for commentary on material marked by an asterisk.

CÉSAR VALLEJO

II

Tiempo Tiempo.

Mediodía estancado entre relentes.
Bomba aburrida del cuartel achica
tiempo tiempo tiempo tiempo.

Era Era.

Gallos cancionan escarbando en vano.
Boca del claro día que conjuga.
era era era era.

Mañana Mañana.

El reposo caliente aún de ser.
Piensa el presente guárdame para
mañana mañana mañana mañana.

Nombre Nombre.

¿Qué se llama cuanto heriza nos?
Se llama Lomismo que padece
nombre nombre nombre nombrE.

4

II

Time Time.

Noon dammed up in night damp.
Bored pump in the cell block bailing out
time time time time.

Was Was.

Cocks song on scratching in vain.   *
Mouth of the bright day that conjugates
was was was was.

Tomorrow Tomorrow.

The repose in being still warm.
The present thinks keep me for
tomorrow tomorrow tomorrow tomorrow.

Name Name.

What call all that stands our end on hAIR?   *
It's called Thesame that suffers
name name name namE.

III

Las personas mayores
¿a qué hora volverán?
Da las seis el ciego Santiago,
y ya está muy oscuro.

Madre dijo que no demoraría.

Aguedita, Nativa, Miguel,
cuidado con ir por ahí, por donde
acaban de pasar gangueando sus memorias
dobladoras penas,
hacia el silencioso corral, y por donde
las gallinas que se están acostando todavía,
se han espantado tánto.
Mejor estemos aquí no más.
Madre dijo que no demoraría.

Ya no tengamos pena. Vamos viendo
los barcos ¡el mío es más bonito de todos!
con los cuales jugamos todo el santo día,
sin pelearnos, como debe de ser:
han quedado en el pozo de agua, listos,
fletados de dulces para mañana.

Aguardemos así, obedientes y sin más

III

The grown-ups
—when are they coming back?
Blind Santiago is ringing six o'clock,   *
and it's already pretty dark.

Mother said she wouldn't be late.

Aguedita, Nativa, Miguel,   *
be careful going around there, where
stooped souls in torment   *
have just passed twanging their memories,
toward the silent barnyard, and where
the hens still getting settled,
had been so frightened.
We'd better stay right here.
Mother said she wouldn't be late.

We shouldn't fret. Let's keep looking at
the boats—mine's the nicest of all!   .
we've been playing with all day long,
without fighting, how it should be:
they've stayed on the well water, ready,
loaded with candy for tomorrow.

So let's wait, obedient and with no

remedio, la vuelta, el desagravio
de los mayores siempre delanteros
dejándonos en casa a los pequeños,
como si también nosotros
                              no pudiésemos partir.

Aguedita, Nativa Miguel?
Llamo, busco al tanteo en la oscuridad.
No me vayan a haber dejado solo,
y el único recluso sea yo.

other choice, for the return, the apologies
of the grown-ups always in front
leaving us the little ones at home
as if we too couldn't

        go away.

    Aguedita, Nativa, Miguel?
I call out, I grope in the dark.
They can't have left me all alone,
the only prisoner can't be me.

IV

Rechinan dos carretas contra los martillos
hasta los lagrimales trifurcas,
cuando nunca las hicimos nada.
A aquella otra sí, desamada,
amargurada bajo túnel campero
por lo uno, y sobre duras áljidas
pruebas   espiritivas.

Tendíme en són de tercera parte,
mas la tarde—qué la bamos a hhazer—
se anilla en mi cabeza, furiosamente
a no querer dosificarse en madre. Son
*   los anillos.*
Son los nupciales trópicos ya tascados.
El alejarse, mejor que todo,
rompe a Crisol.

Aquel no haber descolorado
por nada. Lado al lado al destino y llora
y llora. Toda la canción
cuadrada en tres silencios.

Calor. Ovario. Casi trañsparencia.
Háse llorado todo.   Háse entero velado
en plena izquierda.

IV

Two carts grind against the hammers
until trifurca lachrymals,   *
when we never did anything to them.
To that other one yes, unloved,
embitternessed under an unsheltered tunnel   *
by the first one, and over tough aljid
spiritive   ·   ordeals.   *

I stretched out as a third part,
but the evening—what'her we gonna dooo—   *
rings around in my head, furiously
not wanting to double mother's dose. They are   *
                        the rings.
They are the nuptial tropics already browsed.
The parting, best of all,
breaks into Crucible.

That one that nothing had
discolored. Side to side to destiny and cries
and cries. The whole song
squared by three silences.

Heat. Ovary. Almost transparency.
All has been cried out.   Has been completely veiled
in deep left.

V

*Grupo dicotiledón. Oberturan
desde él petreles, propensiones de trinidad,
finales que comienzan, ohs de ayes
creyérase avaloriados de heterogeneidad.
¡Grupo de los dos cotiledones!*

*A ver. Aquello sea sin ser más.
A ver. No trascienda hacia afuera,
y piense en són de no ser escuchado,
y crome y·no sea visto.
Y no glise en el gran colapso.*

*La creada voz rebélase y no quiere
ser malla, ni amor.
Los novios sean novios en eternidad.
Pues no deis 1, que resonará al infinito.
Y no deis 0, que callará tánto,
hasta despertar y poner de pie al 1.*

Ah grupo bicardiaco.

V

Dicotyledonous group. From it
petrels overture, propensities for trinity,
finales that begin, ohs of ayes
believed to be rhinestoned with heterogeneity.   *
Group of the two cotyledons!

    Let's see. That one could be without being more.
Let's see. Don't let it transcend outward,
and think as if it's not being listened to,
and chrome and not be seen.
And not glise on the great collapse.   *

    The created voice rebels and doesn't want
to be chainmail, or amour.
Let the newlyweds be newlyweds in eternity.
So dont strike 1, which will echo into infinity.
And don't strike 0, which will be so still,
until it wakes the 1 and makes it stand.

    Ah bicardiac group.

VI

El traje que vestí mañana
no lo ha lavado mi lavandera:
lo lavaba en sus venas otilinas,
en el chorro de su corazón, y hoy no he
de preguntarme si yo dejaba
el traje turbio de injusticia.

A hora que no hay quien vaya a las aguas,
en mis falsillas encañona
el lienzo para emplumar, y todas las cosas
del velador de tánto qué será de mí,
todas no están mías
a mi lado.
                    Quedaron de su propiedad,
fratesadas, selladas con su trigueña bondad.

Y si supiera si ha de volver;
y si supiera qué mañana entrará
a entregarme las ropas lavadas, mi aquella
lavandera del alma. Qué mañana entrará
satisfecha, capulí de obrería, dichosa
de probar que sí sabe, que sí puede
                    ¡COMO NO VA A PODER!
azular y planchar todos los caos.

VI

The suit I wore tomorrow
my laundress has not laundered it:
she used to launder it in her Otilian veins,   *
in the gush of her heart, and today I don't
have to wonder if I left
the suit muddy with injustice.

Now that there's no one who goes to the waters,
the linen for feathering
fledges in my underlining, and all the things
on the night stand from so much what'll become of me,
all don't feel mine
at my side.
                    They remained her property,
lustred, sealed with her olive-skinned goodness.   *

And if only I knew she'd come back;
and if only I knew what morning she'd come in
to hand me my laundered clothes, my own that
laundress of the soul. What morning she'd come in
satisfied, a tawny berry of handiwork, happy   *
to prove that yes she does know, that yes she can
                    HOW COULD SHE NOT!
bleach and iron all the chaoses.

VII

Rumbé sin novedad por la veteada calle
que yo me sé. Todo sin novedad,
de veras. Y fondeé hacia cosas así,
y fuí pasado.

Doblé la calle por la que raras
veces se pasa con bien, salida
heroica por la herida de aquella
esquina viva, nada a medias.

Son los grandores,
el grito aquel, la claridad de careo,
la barreta sumersa en su función de
                              ¡ya!
Cuando la calle está ojerosa de puertas,
y pregona desde descalzos atriles
trasmañanar las salvas en los dobles.

Ahora hormigas minuteras
se adentran dulzoradas, dormitadas, apenas
dispuestas, y se baldan,
quemadas pólvoras, altos de a 1921.

VII

I headed as usual down the veined street
I know so well. Everything as usual,
really. And I sounded toward things in this way,
and was past.

I turned onto the street on which one
rarely fares well, an heroic
exit through the wound of that
raw corner, nothing halfway.

They are the magnitudes,
that shout, the clarity of facing off,
the pickaxe plunged into its function of
                        now!
When the street is hollow-eyed with doors,
and proclaims from barefoot lecterns
procrastinating the salvos in the knells.

Now minute hand ants
penetrate deep ensweetened, drowsy, barely
groomed, and spend themselves,
burnt-out powder, the upstairs price 1921.

VIII

Mañana esotro día, alguna
vez hallaría para el hifalto poder,
entrada eternal.

Mañana algún día,
sería la tienda chapada
con un par de pericardios, pareja
de carnívoros en celo.

Bien puede afincar todo eso.
Pero un mañana sin mañana,
entre los aros de que enviudemos,
margen de espejo habrá
donde traspasaré mi propio frente
hasta perder el eco
y quedar con el frente hacia la espalda.

VIII

Tomorrow that other day, some-
time I might find for the saltatory power,   *
eternal entrance.

Tomorrow someday,
the shop might be plated
with a pair of pericardiums, paired
carnivores in rut.

Could very well take root all this.
But one tomorrow without tomorrow,
between the rings of which we become widowers,
a margin of mirror there will be
where I run through my own front
until the echo is lost
and I'm left with the front toward my back.

IX

Vusco volvvver de golpe el golpe.
Sus dos hojas anchas, su válvula
que se abre en suculenta recepción
de multiplicando a multiplicador,
su condición excelente para el placer,
todo avía verdad.

Busco volvver de golpe el golpe.
A su halago, enveto bolivarianas fragosidades
a treintidós cables y sus múltiples,
se arrequintan pelo por pelo
soberanos belfos, los dos tomos de la Obra,
y no vivo entonces ausencia,
*   ni al tacto.*

Fallo bolver de golpe el golpe.
No ensillaremos jamás el toroso Vaveo
de egoísmo y de aquel ludir mortal
de sábana,
desque la mujer esta
*   ¡cuánto pesa de general!*

Y hembra es el alma de la ausente.
Y hembra es el alma mía.

IX   *

I sdrive to dddeflect at a blow the blow.
Her two broad leaves, her valve
opening in succulent reception
from multiplicand to multiplier,
her condition excellent for pleasure,
all readies truth.   *

I strive to ddeflect at a blow the blow.
To her flattery, I transasfixiate Bolivarian asperities   *
at thirty-two cables and their multiples,
hair for hair majestic thick lips,
the two tomes of the Work, constringe,
and I do not live absence then,
                    not even by touch.

I fail to teflect at a blow the blow.
We will never saddle the torose Trool
of egotism or of that mortal chafe
of the bedsheet,
since this here woman
          —what weight as general!

And female is the soul of the absent-she.
And female is my own soul.

X

Prístina y última piedra de infundada
ventura, acaba de morir
con alma y todo, octubre habitación y encinta.
De tres meses de ausente y diez de dulce.
Cómo el destino,
mitrado monodáctilo, ríe.

Cómo detrás desahucian juntas
de contrarios. Cómo siempre asoma el guarismo
bajo la línea de todo avatar.

Cómo escotan las ballenas a palomas.
Cómo a su vez éstas dejan el pico
cubicado en tercera ala.
Cómo arzonamos, cara a monótonas ancas.

Se remolca diez meses hacia la decena,
hacia otro más allá.
Dos quedan por lo menos todavía en pañales.
Y los tres meses de ausencia.
Y los nueve de gestación.

No hay ni una violencia,
El paciente incorpórase,
y sentado empavona tranquilas misturas.

X

The pristine and last stone of groundless
fortune, has just died
with soul and all, October bedroom and pregnant.
Of three months of absent and ten of sweet.
How destiny,
mitred monodactyl, laughs.

How at the rear conjunctions of contraries
destroy all hope. How under every avatar's lineage
the number always shows up.

How whales cut doves to fit.
How these in turn leave their beak
cubed as a third wing.
How we saddleframe, facing monotonous croups.

Ten months are towed toward the tenth,
toward another beyond.
Two at least are still in diapers.
And the three months of absence.
And the nine of gestation.

There's not even any violence.
The patient raises up,
and seated enpeacocks tranquil nosegays.

XI

He encontrado a una niña
en la calle, y me ha abrazado.
Equis, disertada, quien la halló y la halle,
no la va a recordar.

Esta niña es mi prima. Hoy, al tocarle
el talle, mis manos han entrado en su edad
como en par de mal rebocados sepulcros.
Y por la misma desolación marchóse,
delta al sol tenebloso,
trina entre los dos.

"Me he casado",
me dice. Cuando lo que hicimos de niños
en casa de la tía difunta.
Se ha casado.
Se ha casado.

Tardes años latitudinales,
qué verdaderas ganas nos ha dado
de jugar a los toros, a las yuntas,
pero todo de engaños, de candor, como fué.

XI

I have met a girl
in the street, and she has embraced me.
X, expounded, whoever found her and finds her,
will not remember her.

   This girl is my cousin. Today, on touching
her waist, my hands have entered her age
as into a pair of badly plasdered tombs.
And for that very desolation she left,
               the delta in a tenebrus sun,
               a trine between the two.

               "I got married,"
she tells me. When what we did as kids
in the house of our dead aunt.
                    She's married.
                    She's married.

   Late latitudinal years,
how much it made us want
to play bulls, yoked oxen,
but just fooling, in candor, like it was.

XII

Escapo de una finta, peluza a peluza.
Un proyectil que no sé dónde irá a caer.
Incertidumbre. Tramonto. Cervical coyuntura.

Chasquido de moscón que muere
a mitad de su vuelo y cae a tierra.
¿Qué dice ahora Newton?
Pero, naturalmente, vosotros sois hijos.

Incertidumbre. Talones que no giran.
Carilla en nudo, fabrida
cinco espinas por un lado
y cinco por el otro: Chit! Ya sale.

XII

I escape from a feint, fluf for fluf.
A projectile I know not where it will fall.
Incertitude. Tramontation. Cervical articulation.   *

Zap of a horsefly that dies
in mid-air and drops to earth.
What would Newton say now?
But, naturally, you're all sons.

Incertitude. Heels that don't spin.
The knotted page, factures   *
five thorns on one side
and five on the other: Ssh! Here it comes.

XIII

Pienso en tu sexo.
Simplificado el corazón, pienso en tu sexo,
ante el hijar maduro del día.
Palpo el botón de dicha, está en sazón.
Y muere un sentimiento antiguo
degenerado en seso.

Pienso en tu sexo, surco más prolífico
y armonioso que el vientre de la Sombra,
aunque la Muerte concibe y pare
de Dios mismo.
Oh Conciencia,
pienso, sí, en el bruto libre
que goza donde quiere, donde puede.

Oh, escándalo de miel de los crepúsculos.
Oh estruendo mudo.

Odumodneurtse!

XIII

I think about your sex.
My heart simplified, I think about your sex,
before the ripe daughterloin of day.   *
I touch the bud of joy, it is in season.
And an ancient sentiment dies
degenerated into brains.

I think about your sex, furrow more prolific
and harmonious than the belly of the Shadow,
though Death conceives and bears
from God himself.
Oh Conscience,
I am thinking, yes, about the free beast
who takes pleasure where he wants, where he can.

Oh, scandal of the honey of twilights.
Oh mute thunder.

Rednuhtetum!

XIV

Cual mi explicación.
Esto me lacera de tempranía.

Esa manera de caminar por los trapecios.

Esos corajosos brutos como postizos.

Esa goma que pega el azogue al adentro.

Esas posaderas sentadas para arriba.

Ese no puede ser, sido.

Absurdo.

Demencia.

Pero he venido de Trujillo a Lima.
Pero gano un sueldo de cinco soles.

XIV

As for my explanation.
This lacerates me from earliness.

That way of traveling through trapezes.

Those fitful beasts like toupees.

That rubber that sticks the quicksilver inside.   *

Those buttocks seated upward.

That cannot be, been.

Absurd.

Dementia.

But I have come from Trujillo to Lima.
But I earn a wage of five soles.   *

XV

En el rincón aquel, donde dormimos juntos
tantas noches, ahora me he sentado
a caminar. La cuja de los novios difuntos
fué sacada, o talvez qué habrá pasado.

Has venido temprano a otros asuntos,
y ya no estás. Es el rincón
donde a tu lado, leí una noche,
entre tus tiernos puntos,
un cuento de Daudet. Es el rincón
amado. No lo equivoques.

Me he puesto a recordar los días
de verano idos, tu entrar y salir,
poca y harta y pálida por los cuartos.

En esta noche pluviosa,
ya lejos de ambos dos, salto de pronto...
Son dos puertas abriéndose cerrándose,
dos puertas que al viento van y vienen
sombra   a   sombra.

XV

In that corner, where we slept together
so many nights, I've now sat down
to wander. The deceased newlyweds' bed   *
was taken out, or maybe what will've happened.

You've come early on other matters,
and now you're not around. It is the corner
where at your side, I read one night,
between your tender points,
a story by Daudet. It is the corner   *
we loved. Don't mistake it.

I've started to remember the days
of summer gone, your entering and leaving,
scant and burdened and pale through the rooms.

On this rainy night,
now far from both, I suddenly start...
Two doors are opening closing,   °
two doors that come and go in the wind
shadow   to   shadow.

XVI

Tengo fe en ser fuerte.
Dame, aire manco, dame ir
galoneándome de ceros a la izquierda.
Y tú, sueño, dame tu diamante implacable,
tu tiempo de deshora.

Tengo fe en ser fuerte.
Por allí avanza cóncava mujer,
cantidad incolora, cuya
gracia se cierra donde me abro.

Al aire, fray pasado. Cangrejos, zote!
Avístase la verde bandera presidencial,
arriando las seis banderas restantes,
todas las colgaduras de la vuelta.

Tengo fe en que soy,
y en que he sido menos.

Ea! Buen primero!

XVI

I have faith in being strong.
Give me, armless air, give me leave
to galloon myself with zeros on the left.   *
And you, dream, give me your implacable diamond,
your untimely time.

I have faith in being strong.
Over there advances a concave woman,
a colorless quantity, whose
grace closes where I open.

Into the air, friar past. Dunce, lice!   *
The green presidential flag is glimpsed,
hauling down the six remaining flags,
all the hangings of the return.

I have faith that I am,
and that I've been less.

Hey! A good start!

XVII

Destílase este 2 en una sola tanda,
y entrambos lo apuramos.
Nadie me hubo oído. Estría urente
abracadabra civil.

La mañana no palpa cual la primera,
cual la última piedra ovulandas
a fuerza de secreto. La mañana descalza.
El barro a medias
entre sustancias gris, más y menos.

Caras no saben de la cara, ni de la
marcha a los encuentros.
Y sin hacia cabecee el exergo.
Yerra la punta del afán.

Junio, eres nuestro. Junio, y en tus hombros
me paro a carcajear, secando
mi metro y mis bolsillos
en tus 21 uñas de estación.

Buena! Buena!

XVII

This 2 distills in a single batch,
and together we'll finish it off.
No one'd heard me. Urent groove
civil abracadabra.

The morning doesn't touch like the first,
like the last stone ovulatable   *
by force of secrecy. The morning takes off its shoes.
The mud halfway
between grey matters, more and less.

Faces do not know of the face, nor of the
walk to the rendezvous.
And without a toward the exergue may nod.
The tip of fervor wanders.

June, you're ours. June, and on your shoulders
I stand up to guffaw, drying
my meter and my pockets
on your 21 fingernailed season.

Good! Good!

XVIII

Oh las cuatro paredes de la celda.
Ah las cuatro paredes albicantes
que sin remedio dan al mismo número.

Criadero de nervios, mala brecha,
por sus cuatro rincones cómo arranca
las diarias aherrojadas extremidades.

Amorosa llavera de innumerables llaves,
si estuvieras aquí, si vieras hasta
qué hora son cuatro estas paredes.
Contra ellas seríamos contigo, los dos,
más dos que nunca. Y ni lloraras,
di, libertadora!

Ah las paredes de la celda.
De ellas me duelen entre tanto, más
las dos largas que tienen esta noche
algo de madres que ya muertas
llevan por bromurados declives,
a un niño de la mano cada una.

Y sólo yo me voy quedando,
con la diestra, que hace por ambas manos,

XVIII

Oh the four walls of the cell.
Ah the four bleaching walls
that inevitably face the same number.

Breeding place for nerves, foul breach,
through its four corners how it snatches at
the daily shackled extremities.

Loving keeper of innumerable keys,
if only you were here, if you could only see unto
what hour these walls remain four.
Against them we would be with you, the two of us,
more two than ever. And you wouldn't even cry,
speak, liberator!

Ah the walls of the cell.
Meanwhile of those that hurt me, most
the two long ones that tonight are
somehow like mothers now dead
leading a child through
bromowalled inclines by the hand.

And only I hang on,
with my right, serving for both hands,

en alto, en busca de terciario brazo
que ha de pupilar, entre mi donde y mi cuando,
esta mayoría inválida de hombre.

raised, in search of a tertiary arm
to pupilize, between my where and my when,
this invalid majority of a man.

XIX

A trastear, Hélpide dulce, escampas,
cómo quedamos de tan quedarnos.

Hoy vienes apenas me he levantado.
El establo está divinamente meado
y excrementido por la vaca inocente
y el inocente asno y el gallo inocente.

Penetra en la maría ecuménica.
Oh sangabriel, has que conciba el alma,
el sin luz amor, el sin cielo,
lo más piedra, lo más nada,
          hasta la ilusión monarca.

Quemaremos todas las naves!
Quemaremos la última esencia!

Mas si se ha de sufrir de mito a mito,
y a hablarme llegas masticando hielo,
mastiquemos brasas,
ya no hay donde bajar,
ya no hay donde subir.

Se ha puesto el gallo incierto, hombre.

XIX   *

To descant, sweet Hélpide, you babble,   *
how we remain from so remaining ourselves.

Today you came just when I got up.
The stable has been divinely pissed
and defacated by the innocent cow
and the innocent ass and the innocent cock.

Penetrate into the ecumenical mary.
Oh saintgabriel, make the soul conceive,
the lightless love, the heavenless,
that most stone, that most nothing,
        even the monarch illusion.

Let's burn all the bridges!
Let's burn the ultimate essence!

But if one is to suffer from myth to myth,
and to speak to me you arrive chewing ice,
let's chew embers,
now there is no where to descend,
now there is no where to rise.

The cock has become uncertain, man.

XX

Al ras de batiente nata blindada
de piedra ideal. Pues apenas
acerco el 1 al 1 para no caer.

Ese hombre mostachoso. Sol,
herrada su única rueda, quinta y perfecta,
y desde ella para arriba.
Bulla de botones de bragueta,
                    libres,
bulla que reprende A vertical subordinada.
El desagüe jurídico. La chirota grata.

Mas sufro. Allende sufro. Aquende sufro.

Y he aquí se me cae la baba, soy
una bella persona, cuando
el hombre guillermosecundario
puja y suda felicidad
a chorros, al dar lustre al calzado
de su pequeña de tres años.

Engállase el barbado y frota un lado.
La niña en tanto pónese el índice
en la lengua que empieza a deletrear
los enredos de enredos de los enredos,

XX

Flush with bubbling milk scum buttressed
by ideal stone. Thus barely do
I bring 1 up to 1 so as to not fall.

That mustachioed man. Sun,
its only wheel iron-rimmed, fifth and perfect,
and from it on upward.
Bustle of crotch buttons,
          free,
bustle that reprimands A subordinate vertical.
Juridical drainage. Grateful gullery.   *

But I suffer. Thither I suffer. Hither I suffer.

And behold I am a doting fool, I am
a beautiful person, when
the williamthesecondary man
strains, drip-happy
with sweat, while putting a shine
on his little three year old's shoe.

Whiskers puffs himself up and rubs one side.
The girl meanwhile puts her forefinger
on her tongue which starts spelling
the tangles of the tangles of the tangles,

y unta el otro zapato, a escondidas,
con un poquito de saliba y tierra,
pero con un poquito
no má-

.s.

and dabs the other shoe, secretly,
with a bit of sylliva and dirt,
                    but just a bit,
                    no mor-
                        .e.

XXI

En un auto arteriado de círculos viciosos,
torna diciembre qué cambiado,
con su oro en desgracia. Quién le viera:
diciembre con sus 31 pieles rotas,
               el pobre diablo.

Yo le recuerdo. Hubimos de esplendor,
bocas ensortijadas de mal engreimiento,
todas arrastrando recelos infinitos.
Cómo no voy a recordarle
al magro señor Doce.

Yo le recuerdo. Y hoy diciembre torna
qué cambiado, el aliento a infortunio,
helado, moqueando humillación.

Y a la ternurosa avestruz
como que la que ha querido, como que la ha adorado.
Por ella se ha calzado todas sus diferencias.

XXI

In an auto arteried with vicious circles,   *
December returns so changed,
with his gold in disgrace. Who'd believe it:
December with his 31 skins torn,
                                    the poor devil.

I remember him. We had to splendor,   *
mouths twisted with vain conceit,
everybody dragging infinite distrusts.
How can I not remember
the gaunt Mr. Twelve.

I remember him. And today December returns
so changed, his breath to misfortune,
frozen, blubbering humiliation.

And to the tenderlovin' ostrich
as if he had loved her, as if he had adored her.
For her he has put on all his differences.

XXII

Es posible me persigan hasta cuatro
magistrados vuelto. Es posible me juzguen pedro.
¡Cuatro humanidades justas juntas!
Don Juan Jacobo está en hacerio,
y las burlas le tiran de su soledad,
como a un tonto. Bien hecho.

Farol rotoso, el día induce a darle algo,
y pende
a modo de asterisco que se mendiga
a sí propio quizás qué enmendaturas.

Ahora que chirapa tan bonito
en esta paz de una sola línea,
aquí me tienes,
aquí me tienes, de quien yo penda,
para que sacies mis esquinas.
Y si, éstas colmadas,
te derramases de mayor bondad,
sacaré de donde no haya,
forjaré de locura otros posillos,
insaciables ganas
de nivel y amor.

XXII

Possibly up to four magistrates
pursue me returned. Possibly they'll judge me peter.
Four joined just humanities!
M. Jean Jacques is in the black books,   *
and the jeers draw him out of his solitude,
like a fool. Well done.

A cracked lantern, the day induces to give it something,
and it hangs
like an asterisk begging
from itself who knows what emendations.

Now that it rainshines so pretty   *
in this peace of a single line,
here you have me,
here you have me, from whom I might hang,   .
so that you may satiate my corners.
And if, these brimming,
you overflow with greater kindness,
I'll draw from where there may not be,
I'll forge from madness other sumpz,
insatiable urges
to level and love.

CÉSAR VALLEJO

Si pues siempre salimos al encuentro
de cuanto entra por otro lado,
ahora, chirapado eterno y todo,
heme, de quien yo penda,
estoy de filo todavía. Heme!

If then we always turn to oppose
whatever enters from the other side,
now, rainshone eternal and all,
here I am, from whom I might hang,
I'm edgewise still. Here I am!

XXIII

Tahona estuosa de aquellos mis bizcochos
pura yema infantil innumerable, madre.

Oh tus cuatro gorgas, asombrosamente
mal plañidas, madre: tus mendigos.
Las dos hermanas últimas, Miguel que ha muerto
y yo arrastrando todavía
una trenza por cada letra del abecedario.

En la sala de arriba nos repartías
de mañana, de tarde, de dual estiba,
aquellas ricas hostias de tiempo, para
que ahora nos sobrasen
cáscaras de relojes en flexión de las 24
en punto parados.

Madre, y ahora! Ahora, en cuál alvéolo
quedaría, en qué retoño capilar,
cierta migaja que hoy se me ata al cuello
y no quiere pasar. Hoy que hasta
tus puros huesos estarán harina
que no habrá en qué amasar
¡tierna dulcera de amor!,
hasta en la cruda sombra, hasta en el gran molar
cuya encía late en aquel lácteo hoyuelo

XXIII

Radiant bakery of those my sweet rolls
pure infantile innumerable yolk, mother.

Oh your four gorges, astoundingly
mislamented, mother: your beggars.
The two youngest sisters, Miguel who has died
and me still pulling
one braid for each letter in the primer.

In the room upstairs you handed out to us
morning and evening, from a dual stowage,
those delicious hosts of time, so
that now we'd have more than enough
clock husks in flexion of 24 hours
stopped on the dot.

Mother, and now! Now, in which alveolus
might remain, on what capillary sprout,
a certain crumb that today perplexed in my throat
doesn't want to go down. Today when even
your pure bones might be flour
with nowhere to knead
—tender confectioner of love,
even in raw shade, even in the great molar
whose gum throbs on that lacteal dimple

que inadvertido lábrase y pulula ¡tú lo viste tánto!
en las cerradas manos recién nacidas.

    Tal la tierra oirá en tu silenciar,
cómo nos van cobrando todos
el alquiler del mundo donde nos dejas
y el valor de aquel pan inacabable.
Y nos lo cobran, cuando, siendo nosotros
pequeños entonces, como tú verías,
no se lo podíamos haber arrebatado
a nadie; cuando tú nos lo diste,
¿dí, mamá?

that unseen fabricates and abounds—you saw it so often!
in closed hands newborn.

    So the earth will hear in your silency,   *
how they keep charging us all
rent on the world in which you leave us
and the cost of that interminable bread.
And they charge us for it, when, being only
children then, as you could see,
we couldn't have snatched it
from anyone; when you gave it to us,
no, mama?

XXIV

Al borde de un sepulcro florecido
trascurren dos marías llorando,
llorando a mares.

El ñandú desplumado del recuerdo
alarga su postrera pluma,
y con ella la mano negativa de Pedro
graba en un domingo de ramos
resonancias de exequias y de piedras.

Del borde de un sepulcro removido
se alejan dos marías cantando.

Lunes.

XXIV

By the edge of a flowered tomb
two marys pass weeping,
weeping passionately.

The deplumed nandu of memory
extends its hindmost plume,
and with it Peter's negative hand
engraves on a palm sunday
echoes of exequies and stones.

From the edge of a disturbed tomb
two marys go off singing.

Monday.

XXV

Alfan alfiles a adherirse
a las junturas, al fondo, a los testuces,
al sobrelecho de los numeradores a pie.
Alfiles y cadillos de lupinas parvas.

Al rebufar el socaire de cada caravela
deshilada sin americanizar,
ceden las estevas en espasmo de infortunio,
con pulso párvulo mal habituado
a sonarse en el dorso de la muñeca.
Y la más aguda tiplisonancia
se tonsura y apeálase, y largamente
se ennazala hacia carámbanos
de lástima infinita.

Soberbios lomos resoplan
al portar, pendientes de mustios petrales,
las escarapelas con sus siete colores
bajo cero, desde las islas guaneras
hasta las islas guaneras.
Tal los escarzos a la intemperie de pobre
fe.
Tal el tiempo de las rondas. Tal el del rodeo
para los planos futuros,

XXV

Thrips uprear to adhere   *
to joints, to the base, to napes,
to the underface of numerators on foot.
Thrips and thrums from lupine heaps.

As the lee of each caravel, unraveled
without Americanizing, snorts loudly,
carriage perches collapse in a calamitous spasm,
with a puny pulse unfortunately given
to blowing its nose on the back of its wrist.
And the most high-pitched sopraneity
tonsures and hobbles itself, and gradually
ennasals toward icicles   *
of infinite pity.

Spirited loins wheeze hard
on bearing, dangling from musty breastplates,
cockades with their seven colors
below zero, from the guano islands
to the guano islands.
Thus the dirty honeycombs in the open air of little
faith.
Thus the hour of the rounds. Thus the one with a detour
to future planes,

cuando innánima grifalda relata sólo
fallidas callandas cruzadas.

    Vienen entonces alfiles a adherirse
hasta en las puertas falsas y en los borradores.

when the innanimous gerfalcon reports solely   *
failed silence-deserving crusades.

   Then thrips end up adhering
even in trap doors and in rough drafts.

XXVI

El verano echa nudo a tres años
que, encintados de cárdenas cintas, a todo
        sollozo,
aurigan orinientos índices
de moribundas alejandrías,
de cuzcos moribundos.

   Nudo alvino deshecho, una pierna por allí,
más allá todavía la otra,
            desgajadas,
            péndulas.
Deshecho nudo de lácteas glándulas
de la sinamayera,
bueno para alpacas brillantes,
para abrigo de pluma inservible
¡más piernas los brazos que brazos!

   Así envérase el fin, como todo,
como polluelo adormido saltón
de la hendida cáscara,
a luz eternamente polla.
Y así, desde el óvalo, con cuatros al hombro,
        ya para qué tristura.

   Las uñas aquellas dolían

XXVI

Summer knots three years
that, beribboned with carmine ribbons, at full
        sob,
are charioted by the rusty indices   *
of moribund alexandrias,
of cuzcos moribund.

Alvine knot undone, one leg there,
the other even further,
        torn off,
        pendulous.
Undone knot of the sinamayera's   *
lacteal glands,
good for brilliant alpacas,
for a coat of useless feather
—arms more legs than arms!

So the end shows color, like everything,
like a drowsy chick hopping
from the cracked shell,
into light eternally pullet.
And so, after the ovum, shouldering fours,
        already for what sorrow.

Those fingernails ached

retesando los propios dedos hospicios.
De entonces crecen ellas para adentro,
        mueren para afuera,
        y al medio ni van ni vienen,
        ni van ni vienen.

    Las uñas. Apeona ardiente avestruz coja,
desde perdidos sures,
flecha hasta el estrecho ciego
                    de senos aunados.

    Al calor de una punta
de pobre sesgo ESFORZADO,
la griega sota de oros tórnase
morena sota de islas,
cobriza sota de lagos
en frente a moribunda alejandría,
a cuzco moribundo.

tautening their own asylum fingers.
From then on they grow inward,
        die outward,
        and in between neither come nor go,
        neither come nor go.

    The nails. An ardent crippled ostrich runs,
from lost sures,   *
an arrow into the blind strait
                        of fused breasts.

    In the heat of a point
of VIGOROUS humble obliquity,
the greek jack of diamonds turns into
a swarthy jack of islands,
a coppery jack of lakes
facing moribund alexandria,
cuzco moribund.

XXVII

Me da miedo ese chorro,
buen recuerdo, señor fuerte, implacable
cruel dulzor. Me da miedo.
Esta casa me da entero bien, entero
lugar para este no saber donde estar.

No entremos. Me da miedo este favor
de tornar por minutos, por puentes volados.
Yo no avanzo, señor dulce,
recuerdo valeroso, triste
esqueleto cantor.

Qué contenido, el de esta casa encantada,
me da muertes de azogue, y obtura
con plomo mis tomas
a la seca actualidad.

El chorro que no sabe a cómo vamos,
dame miedo, pavor.
Recuerdo valeroso, yo no avanzo.
Rubio y triste esqueleto, silba, silba.

XXVII

This spurt frightens me,
good memory, powerful master, implacable
cruel sweetness. It frightens me.
This house pleases me perfectly, a perfect
spot for this not knowing where to be.

Let's not go in. It frightens me, this permission
to return by the minute, across exploded bridges.
I push no further, sweet master,
courageous memory, sad
songskeleton.

How the content, that of this enchanted house,
spends my quicksilver, and plugs
with lead my outlets
to dry actuality.

The spurt that doesn't know how we're doing,
frightens me, terrifies me.
Courageous memory, I push no further.
Blond and sad skeleton, whistle, whistle.

XXVIII

He almorzado solo ahora, y no he tenido
madre, ni súplica, ni sírvete, ni agua,
ni padre que, en el facundo ofertorio
de los choclos, pregunte para su tardanza
de imagen, por los broches mayores del sonido.

  Cómo iba yo a almorzar. Cómo me iba a servir
de tales platos distantes esas cosas,
cuando habráse quebrado el propio hogar,
cuando no asoma ni madre a los labios.
Cómo iba yo a almorzar nonada.

  A la mesa de un buen amigo he almorzado
con su padre recién llegado del mundo,
con sus canas tías que hablan
en tordillo retinte de porcelana,
bisbiseando por todos sus viudos alvéolos:
y con cubiertos francos de alegres tiroriros,
porque estánse en su casa. Así, qué gracia!
Y me han dolido los cuchillos
de esta mesa en todo el paladar.

  El yantar de estas mesas así, en que se prueba
amor ajeno en vez del propio amor,
torna tierra el bocado que no brinda la

XXVIII

I've had lunch alone now, and without any
mother, or may I have, or help yourself, or water,
or father who, over the eloquent offertory
of ears of corn, asks for his postponed
image, between the greater clasps of sound.

How could I have had lunch. How served myself
these things from such distant plates,
when my own hearth has surely broken up,
when not even mother appears at my lips.
How could I have had a nothing lunch.

At the table of a good friend I've had lunch
with his father just arrived from the world,
with his white-haired aunts who speak
in dapple-grey tinkle of porcelain,
mumbling through all their widow alveoli;
and with generous place-settings of lively tootlings,
because they're in their own home. What a snap!
And the knives on this table
have hurt me all over my palate.

Viandry at such tables, where one proves   *
someone else's love instead of one's own,
turns into earth the mouthful not offered by

MADRE,
hace golpe la dura deglusión; el dulce,
hiel; aceite funéreo, el café.

Cuando ya se ha quebrado el propio hogar,
y el sírvete materno no sale de la
tumba,
la cocina a oscuras, la miseria de amor.

TRILCE

MOTHER,
makes the hard swalowing a blow; the dessert,
bile; the coffee, funereal oil.

Now when my own hearth has broken up,
and the maternal help yourself does not leave the
tomb,
the kitchen in darkness, the misery of love.

XXIX

Zumba el tedio enfrascado
bajo el momento improducido y caña.

Pasa una paralela a
ingrata línea quebrada de felicidad.
Me extraña cada firmeza, junto a esa agua
que se aleja, que ríe acero, caña.

Hilo retemplado, hilo, hilo binómico
¿por dónde romperás, nudo de guerra?

Acoraza este ecuador, Luna.

XXIX

Bottled tedium buzzes
under the moment unproduced and cane.

A parallel turns into
an ungrateful broken line of joy.
Each steadiness estranges me, next to that water
that recedes, that laughs steel, cane.

Retempered thread, thread, binomic thread
—where will you break, knot of war?

Armor-plate this equator, Moon.

XXX

Quemadura del segundo
en toda la tierna carnecilla del deseo,
picadura de ají vagoroso
a las dos de la tarde inmoral.

Guante de los bordes borde a borde.
Olorosa verdad tocada en vivo, al conectar
la antena del sexo
con lo que estamos siendo sin saberlo.

Lavaza de máxima ablución.
Calderas viajeras
que se chocan y salpican de fresca sombra
unánime, el color, la fracción, la dura vida,
la dura vida eterna.
No temamos. La muerte es así.

El sexo sangre de la amada que se queja
dulzorada, de portar tánto
por tan punto ridículo.
Y el circuito
entre nuestro pobre día y la noche grande,
a las dos de la tarde inmoral.

XXX

Burn of the second
throughout the tender fleshbud of desire,
sting of vagurant chili   *
at two in the immoral afternoon.

Glove of the edges edge to edge.
Aromatic truth touched to the quick, on connecting
the sexual antenna
to what we are being without knowing it.

Slop of maximum ablution.
Voyaging boilers
that crash and spatter with unanimous fresh
shadow, the color, the fraction, the hard life,
            the hard life eternal.
Let's not be afraid. Death is like that.

Sex blood of the beloved who complains
ensweetened, of bearing so much
for such a ridiculous moment.
And the circuit
between our poor day and the great night,
at two in the immoral afternoon.

XXXI

Esperanza plañe entre algodones.

Aristas roncas uniformadas
de amenazas tejidas de esporas magníficas
y con porteros botones innatos.
¿Se luden seis de sol?
Natividad. Cállate, miedo.

Cristiano espero, espero siempre
de hinojos en la piedra circular que está
en las cien esquinas de esta suerte
tan vaga a donde asomo.

Y Dios sobresaltado nos oprime
el pulso, grave, mudo,
y como padre a su pequeña,
                    apenas,
pero apenas, entreabre los sangrientos algodones
y entre sus dedos toma a la esperanza.

Señor, lo quiero yo...
Y basta!

XXXI

Hope wails cotton coddled.   *

Hoarse aristas uniformed
in threats woven of magnificent spores
and with inborn doorman buttons.
Are the six rubbing by sun?
Nativity. Be quiet, fear.

A Christian I hope, hope always
kneeling on the circular stone that is
on the hundred corners of this luck
so vague where I appear.

And God startled presses our
pulse, grave, mute,
and like a father to his little girl,
               just,
but just, opens slightly the bloodied cotton
and takes the hope between his fingers.

Lord, I want it...
And that's enough!

XXXII

999 calorías.
Rumbbb...... Trrraprrrr rrach...... chaz
Serpentínica u del bizcochero
enjirafada al tímpano.

Quién como los hielos. Pero nó.
Quién como lo que va ni más ni menos.
Quién como el justo medio.

1.000 calorías.
Azulea y ríe su gran cachaza
el firmamento gringo. Baja
el sol empavado y le alborota los cascos
al más frío.

Remeda al cuco: Rooooooooeeeis......
tierno autocarril, móvil de sed,
que corre hasta la playa.

Aire, aire! Hielo!
Si al menos el calor(—Mejor
*   no digo nada.*

Y hasta la misma pluma

XXXII

999 calories.
Roombbb...... Hulllablll llust...... ster   *
Serpenteenic e of the sweet roll vendor   *
girafted to the eardrum.   *

Lucky are the ices. But no.
Lucky that which moves neither more nor less.
Lucky the golden mean.

1000 calories.
The gringo firmament looks blue
and chuckles up its hocker. The razzed
sun sets and scrambles the skulls
even of the coldest.

It talks cuckoo talk: Weeeeeetrozzz......
the tender rail car, rolling from thirst,
that runs up to the beach.

Air, air! Ice!
If at least the calor(—Better
                    I say nothing.

And even the very pen

con que escribo por último se troncha.
   Treinta y tres trillones trescientos treinta
y tres calorías.

with which I write finally cracks up.
    Thirty-three trillion three hundred and thirty-three calories.

XXXIII

Si lloviera esta noche, retiraríame
de aquí a mil años.
Mejor a cien no más.
Como si nada hubiese ocurrido, haría
la cuenta de que vengo todavía.

O sin madre, sin amada, sin porfía
de agacharme a aguaitar al fondo, a puro
pulso,
esta noche así, estaría escarmenando
la fibra védica,
la lana védica de mi fin final, hilo
del diantre, traza de haber tenido
por las narices
a dos badajos inacordes de tiempo
en una misma campana.

Haga la cuenta de mi vida,
o haga la cuenta de no haber aún nacido,
no alcanzaré a librarme.

No será lo que aun no haya venido, sino
lo que ha llegado y ya se ha ido,
sino lo que ha llegado y ya se ha ido.

XXXIII

If it should rain tonight, I'd withdraw
from here a thousand years.
Maybe just a hundred.
As if nothing had happened, I'd
imagine that I'm still coming.

Or without mother, without beloved, without persistence
from crouching down to spy at the bottom, with my own
bare hands,
on a night like this, I'd be carding
the Vedic fiber,
the Vedic wool of my endmost end, deuce
of a thread, sign of having led
by their noses
two incordant clappers of time   *
            in the same bell.

However I imagine my life
or imagine not having yet been born,
I will not succeed in freeing myself.

It will not be what is yet to come, but
that which came and already left,
but that which came and already left.

XXXIV

Se acabó el extraño, con quien, tarde
la noche, regresabas parla y parla.
Ya no habrá quien me aguarde,
dispuesto mi lugar, bueno lo malo.

Se acabó la calurosa tarde;
tu gran bahía y tu clamor; la charla
con tu madre acabada
que nos brindaba un té lleno de tarde.

Se acabó todo al fin: las vacaciones,
tu obediencia de pechos, tu manera
de pedirme que no me vaya fuera.

Y se acabó el diminutivo, para
mi mayoría en el dolor sin fin,
y nuestro haber nacido así sin causa.

XXXIV

That's it for the stranger, with whom, late
night, you would return in endless chatter.
Now there will be no one waiting for me,
my place set, what is bad good.

That's it for the glowing evening;
your spacious bay and your outcry; the prattle
with your mother ended
who would offer us a tea full of evening.

That's it for everything at last: the holidays,
your breast-fed obedience, your way
of asking me not to go out.

And that's it for the diminutive, for
my coming of age in unending pain,
and our having been born thus for no reason.

XXXV

El encuentro con la amada
tánto alguna vez, es un simple detalle,
casi un programa hípico en violado,
que de tan largo no se puede doblar bien.

El almuerzo con ella que estaría
poniendo el plato que nos gustara ayer
y se repite ahora,
pero con algo más de mostaza;
el tenedor absorto, su doneo radiante
de pistilo en mayo, y su verecundia
de a centavito, por quítame allá esa paja.
Y la cerveza lírica y nerviosa
a la que celan sus dos pezones sin lúpulo,
y que no se debe tomar mucho!

Y los demás encantos de la mesa
que aquella núbil campaña borda
con sus propias baterías germinales
que han operado toda la mañana,
según me consta, a mí,
amoroso notario de sus intimidades,
y con las diez varillas mágicas
de sus dedos pancreáticos.

XXXV

An hour with the beloved
so much once, is a single detail,
nearly a violet racing-form,
so long that it is hard to fold.

Lunch with her who might be
serving the dish that we liked yesterday
and is repeated today,
but with a bit more mustard;
the absorbed fork, her coquettish radiance
of a pistil in May, and her modesty
worth two cents, to quarrel about a straw.
And the lyric and nervous beer
watched over by her two nipples without hops,
of which you shouldn't drink so much!

And the other bewitchments of the table
which that nubile campaign embroiders
with her own germinal weapons
in operation all morning long,
according to my account, my own,
the amorous notary of her intimacies,
and with the ten magic wands
of her pancreatic fingers.

Mujer que sin pensar en nada más allá,
suelta el mirlo y se pone a conversarnos
sus palabras tiernas
como lancinantes lechugas recién cortadas.

Otro vaso, y me voy. Y nos marchamos,
ahora sí, a trabajar.

Entre tanto, ella se interna
entre los cortinajes y ¡oh aguja de mis días
desgarrados! se sienta a la orilla
de una costura, a coserme el costado
a su costado,
a pegar el botón de esa camisa,
que se ha vuelto a caer. Pero hase visto!

A woman who without a further thought,
starts chattering and begins to engage us
her words tender
as lancinating freshly-cut lettuce.

Another glass, and I'm off. And we leave,
now for sure, to work.

Meanwhile, she takes refuge
behind the curtains and—oh needle of my ripped
days! sits down at the edge
of a seam, to sew my side
to her side,
to stick the button on that shirt,
that's fallen off again. Why fancy that!

XXXVI

Pugnamos ensartarnos por un ojo de aguja,
enfrentados, a las ganadas.
Amoniácase casi el cuarto ángulo del círculo.
¡Hembra se continúa el macho, a raíz
de probables senos, y precisamente
a raíz de cuanto no florece!

¿Por ahí estás, Venus de Milo?
Tú manqueas apenas, pululando
entrañada en los brazos plenarios
de la existencia,
de esta existencia que todaviiza
perenne imperfección.
Venus de Milo, cuyo cercenado, increado
brazo revuélvese y trata de encodarse
a través de verdeantes guijarros gagos,
ortivos nautilos, aunes que gatean
recién, vísperas inmortales.
Laceadora de inminencias, laceadora
del paréntesis.

Rehusad, y vosotros, a posar las plantas
en la seguridad dupla de la Armonía.
Rehusad la simetría a buen seguro.
Intervenid en el conflicto

XXXVI

We struggle to thread ourselves through a needle's eye,
face to face, hellbent on winning.   *
The fourth angle of the circle ammoniafies almost.   *
Female is continued the male, on the basis
of probable breasts, and precisely
on the basis of how much does not flower!

    Are you that way, Venus de Milo?
You hardly act crippled, pullulating
enwombed in the plenary arms
of existence,
of this existence that neverthelessez   *
perpetual imperfection.
Venus de Milo, whose cut off, increate
arm swings round and tries to elbow
across greening stuttering pebbles,
ortive nautili, recently crawling
evens, immortal on the eves of.
Lassoer of imminences, lassoer
of the parenthesis.

    Refuse, all of you, to set foot
on the double security of Harmony.
Truly refuse symmetry.
Intervene in the conflict

de puntas que se disputan
en la más torionda de las justas
el salto por el ojo de la aguja!

    Tal siento ahora al meñique
demás en la siniestra. Lo veo y creo
no debe serme, o por lo menos que está
en sitio donde no debe.
Y me inspira rabia y me azarea
y no hay cómo salir de él, sino haciendo
la cuenta de que hoy es jueves.

¡Ceded al nuevo impar

                potente de orfandad!

of points that contend
in the most rutty of jousts
for the leap through the needle's eye!

So now I feel my little finger
moreover on my left. I see it and think
it shouldn't be me, or at least that it's
in a place where it shouldn't.
And it inspires me with rage and alarms me
and there is no way out of it, except by
pretending that today is Thursday.

Make way for the new odd number
                        potent with orphanhood!

XXXVII

He conocido a una pobre muchacha
a quien conduje hasta la escena.
La madre, sus hermanas qué amables y también
aquel su infortunado "tú no vas a volver".

Como en cierto negocio me iba admirablemente,
me rodeaban de un aire de dinasta florido.
La novia se volvía agua,
y cuán bien me solía llorar
su amor mal aprendido.

Me gustaba su tímida marinera
de humildes aderezos al dar las vueltas,
y cómo su pañuelo trazaba puntos,
tildes, a la melografía de su bailar de juncia.

Y cuando ambos burlamos al párroco,
quebróse mi negocio y el suyo
y la esfera barrida.

XXXVII

I used to know a poor girl
who I brought onto the scene.
The mother, her sisters so nice and likewise
that unfortunate "you're not coming back" of hers.

As I was doing splendidly in a certain business,
they surrounded me with airs of an affluent dynast.
My girlfriend turned to water,
and how well she used to sob for me
her half-learned love.

I enjoyed her bashful marinera   *
of humble adornments circling about,
and how her kerchief would sketch dots,
accents, to the melography of her sedge-like sway.

And when we both sidestepped the priest,
my business failed as did hers
and the sphere swept away.

XXXVIII

Este cristal aguarda ser sorbido
en bruto por boca venidera
sin dientes. No desdentada.
Este cristal es pan no venido todavía.

Hiere cuando lo fuerzan
y ya no tiene cariños animales.
Mas si se le apasiona, se melaría
y tomaría la horma de los sustantivos
que se adjetivan de brindarse.

Quienes lo ven allí triste individuo
incoloro, lo enviarían por amor,
por pasado y a lo más por futuro:
si él no dase por ninguno de sus costados;
si él espera ser sorbido de golpe
y en cuanto transparencia, por boca venidera que ya no tendrá dientes.

Este cristal ha pasado de animal,
y márchase ahora a formar las izquierdas,
los nuevos Menos.
Déjenlo solo no más.

XXXVIII

This crystal waits to be sipped
in the rough by a future mouth
without teeth. Not toothless.
This crystal is bread yet to come.

It wounds when they force it
and no longer shows animal affection.
But if it is excited, it might boil clear
and become a sugar mold for substantives
which adjectivize in self-offerings.

Those who see it there a sad colorless
individual, could dispatch it for love,
through the past and at most into the future:
if it does not surrender any of its sides;
if it waits to be sipped in a gulp
and once transparent, by a future mouth at will no longer have teeth.

This crystal has passed from animal,
and now goes off to form lefts,
the new Minuses.
Just leave it alone.

XXXIX

Quién ha encendido fósforo!
Mésome. Sonrío
a columpio por motivo.
Sonrío aún más, si llegan todos
a ver las guías sin color
y a mí siempre en punto. Qué me importa.

Ni ese bueno del Sol que, al morirse de gusto,
lo desposta todo para distribuirlo
entre las sombras, el pródigo,
ni él me esperaría a la otra banda.
Ni los demás que paran sólo
entrando y saliendo.

Llama con toque de retina
el gran panadero. Y pagamos en señas
curiosísimas el tibio valor innegable
horneado, trascendiente.
Y tomamos el café, ya tarde,
con deficiente azúcar que ha faltado,
y pan sin mantequilla. Qué se va a hacer.

Pero, eso sí, los aros receñidos, barreados.
La salud va en un pie. De frente: marchen!

XXXIX

Who's lit a match!
I yank out. I smile   *
on a swing for a reason.
I smile even more, if all come
to see the colorless guides
and to me always on the dot. What do I care.

Not that good old Sun that, dying of delight,
butchers everything to distribute it
among the shadows, the prodigal,
not even he would await me on the other shore.
Nor the others who end up solely
entering and leaving.

The great baker calls with a tap
on the retina. And we pay with most
curious signs the tepid undeniable baked,
transcendent price.
And we take our coffee, now late,
with deficient sugar that's run out,
and bread without butter. What can one do.

But, of course, the regirded, barred rings.
Health goes on one foot. Forward: march!

XL

Quién nos hubiera dicho que en domingo
así, sobre arácnidas cuestas
se encabritaría la sombra de puro frontal.
(Un molusco ataca yermos ojos encallados,
a razón de dos o más posibilidades tantálicas
contra medio estertor de sangre remordida).

Entonces, ni el propio revés de la pantalla
deshabitada enjugaría las arterias
trasdoseadas de dobles todavías.
Como si nos hubiesen dejado salir! Como
si no estuviésemos embrazados siempre
a los dos flancos diarios de la fatalidad!

Y cuánto nos habríamos ofendido.
Y aún lo que nos habríamos enojado y peleado
y amistado otra vez
y otra vez.

Quién hubiera pensado en tal domingo,
cuando, a rastras, seis codos lamen
de esta manera, hueras yemas lunesentes.

Habríamos sacado contra él, de bajo
de las dos alas del Amor,

XL

Who would have told us that on a Sunday
like this, over arachnoid slopes
the shadow would rear completely frontal.
(A mollusc is attacking barren foundered eyes,
at the rate of two or more tantalean possibilities
against a half death rattle of remorseful blood).

Then, not even the very back of the uninhabited
screen could wipe dry the arteries
extradosed with double neverthelesses.
As if they would have let us leave! As
if we weren't always meshed
at the two daily flanks of fatality!

And how much we might have offended each other.
And yet how much we might have annoyed each other and
fought and made up again
and again.

Who would have thought of such a Sunday,
when, dragging, six elbows are licking
this way, addled Mondayescent yolks.   *

We might have pulled out against it, from under
the two wings of Love,

lustrales plumas terceras, puñales,
nuevos pasajes de papel de oriente.
Para hoy que probamos si aun vivimos,
casi un frente no más.

lustral third feathers, daggers,
new passages on oriental paper.
For today when we test if we even live,
almost a front at the most.

XLI

La Muerte de rodillas mana
su sangre blanca que no es sangre.
Se huele a garantía.
Pero ya me quiero reir.

Murmúrase algo por allí. Callan.
Alguien silba valor de lado,
y hasta se contaría en par
veintitrés costillas que se echan de menos
entre sí, a ambos costados; se contaría
en par también, toda la fila
de trapecios escoltas.

En tanto, el redoblante policial
(Otra vez me quiero reir)
se desquita y nos tunde a palos,
dale y dale,
de membrana a membrana,
tas
con
tas.

XLI

Death kneeling spills
its white blood that's not blood.
It smells of guarantee.
But now I want to laugh.

Something murmurs over there. They quiet.
Someone whistles courage from the side,
and one could even count by twos
the twenty-three ribs that are missing
among themselves, on both sides; once could also
count by twos, the entire file
of trapezius escorts.

Meanwhile, the policial snare drummer
(Again I want to laugh)
gets even and beats us with a stick,
get moving, get moving,
from membrane to membrane,
slap
for
swap.

XLII

Esperaos. Ya os voy a narrar
todo. Esperaos sossiegue
este dolor de cabeza. Esperaos.

¿Dónde os habéis dejado vosotros
que no haceis falta jamás?

Nadie hace falta! Muy bien

Rosa, entra del último piso.
Estoy niño. Y otra vez rosa:
ni sabes a dónde voy.

¿Aspa la estrella de la muerte?
O son extrañas máquinas cosedoras
dentro del costado izquierdo.
Esperaos otro momento.

No nos ha visto nadie. Pura
búscate el talle.
¡A dónde se han saltado tus ojos!

Penetra reencarnada en los salones
de ponentino cristal. Suena
música exacta casi lástima.

XLII

Wait, all of you. Now I'm going to tell you
everything. All of you wait this headache
may subsside. Wait.

Where have you left yourselves
that you're never needed?

No one's needed! Very good.

Rosa, entering from the top floor.
I feel like a child. And again rosa:
you don't even know where I'm going.

Is the death star reeling?
Or are strange sewing machines
inside the left side.
All of you wait one moment more.

No one has seen us. Pure
search for your waist.
Where have your eyes popped!

Reincarnated enter the parlors
of western crystal. Exact
music plays almost a pity.

Me siento mejor. Sin fiebre, y ferviente.
Primavera. Perú. Abro los ojos.
Ave! No salgas. Dios, como si sospechase
algún flujo sin reflujo ay.

Paletada facial, resbala el telón
cabe las conchas.

Acrisis. Tilia, acuéstate.

I feel better. Without fever, and fervent.
Spring. Peru. I open my eyes.
Ave! Don't leave. God, as if suspecting
some ebbless flow ay.

A facial shovelful, the curtain sweeps
nigh the prompt boxes.

Acrisia. Tilia, go to bed.

XLIII

Quién sabe se va a ti. No le ocultes.
Quién sabe madrugada.
Acaríciale. No le digas nada. Está
duro de lo que se ahuyenta.
Acaríciale. Anda! Cómo le tendrías pena.

Narra que no es posible
todos digan que bueno,
cuando ves que se vuelve y revuelve,
animal que ha aprendido a irse... No?
Sí! Acaríciale. No le arguyas.

Quién sabe se va a ti madrugada.
¿Has contado qué poros dan salida solamente,
y cuáles dan entrada?
Acaríciale. Anda! Pero no vaya a saber
que lo haces porque yo te lo ruego.
Anda!

XLIII

Who knows leaves for you. Don't hide him.
Who knows predawn.
Caress him. Say nothing to him. He is
hard from what is kept at bay.
Caress him. Come on! How you could feel for him.

He narrates it is not possible
all will say that it's ok,
when you see him turn around and return,
an animal that has learned to leave... No?
Yes! Caress him. Don't hassle him.

Who knows leaves for you predawn.
Have you counted which pores allow exit only,
and which ones allow entrance?
Caress him. Go ahead! But he should not know
you're doing this because I beg you to.
Do it!

XLIV

Este piano viaja para adentro,
viaja a saltos alegres.
Luego medita en ferrado reposo,
clavado con diez horizontes.

Adelanta. Arrástrase bajo túneles,
más allá, bajo túneles de dolor,
bajo vértebras que fugan naturalmente.

Otras veces van sus trompas,
lentas asias amarillas de vivir,
van de eclipse,
y se espulgan pesadillas insectiles,
ya muertas para el trueno, heraldo de los génesis.

Piano oscuro ¿a quién atisbas
con tu sordera que me oye,
con tu mudez que me asorda?

Oh pulso misterioso.

XLIV

This piano travels within,
travels by joyful leaps.
Then meditates in ferrate repose,
nailed with ten horizons.

It advances. Drags itself under tunnels,
beyond, under tunnels of pain,
under vertebrae naturally fugacious.

At times its tubes go,
slow asias yellow with living,
they go in eclipse,
and insectile nightmares delouse,
now dead to thunder, the herald of geneses.

Dark piano, on whom do you spy
with your deafness that hears me,
with your muteness that deafens me?

Oh mysterious pulse.

XLV

Me desvinculo del mar
cuando vienen las aguas a mí.

Salgamos siempre. Saboreemos
la canción estupenda, la canción dicha
por los labios inferiores del deseo.
Oh prodigiosa doncellez.
Pasa la brisa sin sal.

A lo lejos husmeo los tuétanos
oyendo el tanteo profundo, a la caza
de teclas de resaca.

Y si así diéramos las narices
en el absurdo,
nos cubriremos con el oro de no tener nada,
y empollaremos el ala aun no nacida
de la noche, hermana
de esta ala huérfana del día,
que a fuerza de ser una ya no es ala.

XLV

I lose contact with the sea
when the waters come to me.

Let us always depart. Let us savor
the stupendous song, the song expressed
by the lower lips of desire.
Oh prodigious maidenhood.
The saltless breeze passes.

In the distance I scent the pith
listening to the deep sounding, in search
of undertow keys.

And if in this way we bang head-on
into the absurd,
we'll cover ourselves with the gold of having nothing,
and will hatch the yet unborn wing
of night, the sister
of this orphan wing of day,
that by dint of being one no longer is a wing.

XLVI

La tarde cocinera se detiene
ante la mesa donde tú comiste;
y muerta de hambre tu memoria viene
sin probar ni agua, de lo puro triste.

Mas, como siempre, tu humildad se aviene
a que le brinden la bondad más triste.
Y no quieres gustar, que ves quien viene
filialmente a la mesa en que comiste.

La tarde cocinera te suplica
y te llora en su delantal que aún sórdido
nos empieza a querer de oirnos tánto.

Yo hago esfuerzos también; porque no hay
valor para servirse de estas aves.
Ah! qué nos vamos a servir ya nada.

XLVI

The evening a cook lingers
before the table where you ate;
and starved to death your memory comes
without even sipping, utterly sad.

But, as usual, your humility agrees
to receive the saddest goodness.
And you refuse to taste, seeing who's coming
filially to the table at which you ate.

The evening a cook implores you
and weeps you in her apron which even if sordid
starts to love us having heard us so much.

I too make an effort; for there is no
courage to help oneself to these birds.
Ah! how can we help ourselves to anything.

XLVII

Ciliado arrecife donde nací,
según refieren cronicones y pliegos
de labios familiares historiados
en segunda gracia.

Ciliado archipiélago, te desislas a fondo,
a fondo, archipiélago mío!
Duras todavía las articulaciones
al camino, como cuando nos instan,
y nosotros no cedemos por nada.

Al ver los párpados cerrados,
implumes mayorcitos, devorando azules bombones,
se carcajean pericotes viejos.
Los párpados cerrados, como si, cuando nacemos
siempre no fuese tiempo todavía.

Se va el altar, el cirio para
que no le pasase nada a mi madre,
y por mí que sería con los años, si Dios
quería, Obispo, Papa, Santo, o talvez
sólo un columnario dolor de cabeza.

Y las manitas que se abarquillan

XLVII

Ciliate reef where I was born,
according to the brief chronicles and papers
of family lips historicized
in second grace.

Ciliate archipelago, you deisland thoroughly,   *
          deeply, my archipelago!
Hard still the articulations
on the road, as when they press us,
and we do not yield at all.

On seeing the closed eyelids,
featherless young men, devouring blue bonbons,
burst out laughing old mice.   *
The closed eyelids, as if, when we are born
it was always not yet time.

The altar goes, the taper so
that nothing happens to my mother,
and so that in time to come I might be, God
willing, a Bishop, a Pope, a Saint, or maybe
only a columnar headache.

And the little hands that curl about

asiéndose de algo flotante,
a no querer quedarse.
Y siendo ya la 1.

grabbing something floating,
not wanting to be left.
It being already 1 o'clock.

XLVIII

Tengo ahora 70 soles peruanos.
Cojo la penúltima moneda, la que suena 69 veces púnicas.
Y he aquí, al finalizar su rol,
quémase toda y arde llameante,
           llameante,
redonda entre mis tímpanos alucinados.

Ella, siendo 69, dase contra 70;
luego escala 71, rebota en 72.
Y así se multiplica y espejea impertérrita
en todos los demás piñones.

Ella, vibrando y forcejeando,
pegando grittttos,
soltando árduos, chisporroteantes silencios,
orinándose de natural grandor,
en unánimes postes surgentes,
acaba por ser todos los guarismos,
           La vida entera.

XLVIII

I now have 70 Peruvian soles.
I clutch the penultimate coin, which sound-
s 69 punic times.
And behold, on finalizing its role,
it burns out completely and burns flaming,
                              flaming,
round between my deluded eardrums.

This coin, being 69, bumps into 70;
then scales 71, bounces on 72.
And so it multiplies and shines unshaken
in all its other pinions.

Vibrating and struggling,
letting out yelllls,
unleashing arduous, scintilating silences,
urinating out of natural grandeur,
on unanimous spouting posts,
it ends up being all numbers,
                        the whole of life.

CÉSAR VALLEJO

XLIX

Murmurado en inquietud, cruzo,
el traje largo de sentir, los lunes
                de la verdad.
Nadie me busca ni me reconoce,
y hasta yo he olvidado
                de quien seré.

Cierta guardarropía, sólo ella, nos sabrá
a todos en las blancas hojas
                de las partidas.
Esa guardarropía, ella sola,
al volver de cada facción,
                de cada candelabro
                ciego de nacimiento.

Tampoco yo descubro a nadie, bajo
este mantillo que iridice los lunes
                de la razón;
y no hago más que sonreir a cada púa
de las verjas, en la loca búsqueda
                del conocido.

Buena guardarropía, ábreme
                tus blancas hojas:
quiero reconocer siquiera al 1,

XLIX

Murmured in anxiety, I cross,
the long suit of feeling, the Mondays
          of truth.
No one looks for me or recognizes me,
and even I have forgotten
          whose I will be.

A certain wardrobe, only it, will know
all of us in the white leaves
          of departures.
That wardrobe, it alone,
on returning from each faction,   ,
          from each candelabrum
          blind from birth.

Nor do I discover anyone, under
this muck that irisizes the Mondays   *
          of reason;
and I no more than smile at each spike
of the gratings, in the insane search
          for the known one.

Good wardrobe, open for me
          your white leaves;
I want to recognize at least the 1,

quiero el punto de apoyo, quiero
           saber de estar siquiera.

   En los bastidores donde nos vestimos,
no hay, no Hay nadie: hojas tan sólo
           de par en par.
Y simpre los trajes descolgándose
por si propios, de perchas
como ductores índices grotescos,
y partiendo sin cuerpos, vacantes,
           hasta el matiz prudente
de un gran caldode alas con causas
y lindes fritas.
Y hasta el hueso!

I want a fulcrum, I want to know about
          being here at least.

   Off stage where we dress,
there's—there Is nobody: only leaves
         wide open.
And always suits slipping down,
by themselves, off coat hooks
like grotesque ductor forefingers,
and departing without bodies, vacant,
        right into the prudent nuance
of a great stock of wings with mashed causes
and fried boundaries.
Right down to the bone!

L

El cancerbero cuatro veces
al día maneja a su candado, abriéndonos
cerrándonos los esternones, en guiños
que entendemos perfectamente.

   Con los fundillos lelos melancólicos,
amuchachado de trascendental desaliño,
parado, es adorable el pobre viejo.
Chancea con los presos, hasta el tope
los puños en las ingles. Y hasta mojarrilla
les roe algún mendrugo; pero siempre
cumpliendo su deber.

   Por entre los barrotes pone el punto
fiscal, inadvertido, izándose en la falangita
del meñique,
a la pista de lo que hablo,
lo que como,
lo que sueño.
Quiere el corvino ya no hayan adentros,
y cómo nos duele esto que quiere el cancerbero.

   Por un sistema de relojería, juega
el viejo inminente, pitagórico!
a lo ancho de las aortas. Y sólo

L

Cerberus four times
a day wields his padlock, opening
closing our breastbones, with winks
we understand perfectly.

With his sad, baggy-assed pants,
boyish in transcendental scruffiness,
standing up, the poor old man is adorable.
He jokes with the prisoners, their groins
brimming with their fists. And even jolly
he gnaws some crust for them; but always
doing his duty.

In between the bars he pokes the fiscal
point, unnoticed, hoisting on the third phalanx
of his little finger,
on the trail of what I say,
what I eat,
what I dream.
This raven doesn't want any inwardness,   *
and how much pain for us is in what Cerberus wants.

Through a clockwork system, the imminent,
Pythagorean! old man plays
widthwise in our aortas. And solely

de tarde en noche, con noche
soslaya alguna su excepción de metal.
Pero, naturalmente,
siempre cumpliendo su deber.

from time to night, at night
he somewhat shirks his exception from metal.
But, naturally,
always doing his duty.

LI

Mentira. Si lo hacía de engaños,
y nada más. Ya está. De otro modo,
también tú vas a ver
cuánto va dolerme el haber sido así.

Mentira. Calla.
Ya está bien.
Como otras veces tú me haces esto mismo,
por eso yo también he sido así.

A mí, que había tánto atisbado si de veras
llorabas,
ya que otras veces sólo te quedaste
en tus dulces pucheros,
a mí, que ni soñé que los creyeses,
me ganaron tus lágrimas.
Ya está.

Mas ya lo sabes: todo fué mentira.
Y si sigues llorando, bueno, pues!
Otra vez ni he de verte cuando juegues.

LI

A lie. I was just pretending,
that's all. And that's it. Otherwise,
you're also going to see
how much having been that way's going to hurt me.

A lie. Ssh.
It's ok now.
Like other times you're doing the same thing to me,
therefore I've also been that way .

Me, always spying to see if you really
were crying,
because at other times you'd go off alone
for your sweet little pouts,
me, who never even dreamed you believed them,
your tears won me over.
So there.

But now you know: it was all a lie.
And if you keep on crying—fine by me!
Next time I won't even watch you when you play.

LII

Y nos levantaremos cuando se nos dé
la gana, aunque mamá toda claror
nos despierte con cantora
y linda cólera materna.
Nosotros reiremos a hurtadillas de esto,
mordiendo el canto de las tibias colchas
de vicuña ¡y no me vayas a hacer cosas!

Los humos de los bohíos ¡ah golfillos
en rama! madrugarían a jugar
a las cometas azulinas, azulantes,
y, apañuscando alfarjes y piedras, nos darían
su estímulo fragante de boñiga,
                            para saearnos
al aire nene que no conoce aún las letras,
a pelearles los hilos.

Otro día querrás pastorear
entre tus huecos onfalóideos
                    ávidas cavernas,
            meses nonos,
                    mis telones.
O querrás acompañar a la anciania
a destapar la toma de un crepúsculo,
para que de día surja

LII

And we'll get up when we feel
like it, even though mama all luminosity
rouses us with melodious
and charming maternal anger.
We'll laugh in secret about this,
biting the edge of the warm vicuña
quilts—and don't do that to me!

Fumes from thatched huts—ah bunch
of scamps! rising early to play
with bluish, bluing kites,
and, copping wainscot and stones, they'd
pungently incite us with cow dung,
                        to draw us out
into kiddy air that doesn't know its letters yet,
to struggle over the strings.

Another time you'll want to pasture
between your omphaloid hollows
                    avid caverns,
            ninth months,
                    my drop curtains.
Or you'll want to accompany old age
to unplug the tap of a dusk,
so that all the water slipping away by night

toda el agua que pasa de noche.
*   Y llegas muriéndote de risa,*
y en el almuerzo musical,
cancha reventada, harina con manteca,
con manteca,
le tomas el pelo al peón decúbito
que hoy otra vez olvida dar los buenos días,
esos sus días, buenos con b de baldío,
que insisten en salirle al pobre
por la culata de la v
dentilabial que vela en él.

surges during the day.
    And you'll arrive dying of laughter,
and at the musical lunch,
popped roasted corn, flour with lard,
with lard,
you'll tease the decubital peasant
who today once again forgets to say buenos días,
those días of his, buenos with the b of barrens,
that keep backfiring for the poor guy
through the dentilabial
v that holds vigil in him. '

LIII

Quién clama las once no son doce!
Como si las hubiesen pujado, se afrotan
de dos en dos las once veces.

Cabezazo brutal. Asoman
las coronas a oir,
pero sin traspasar los eternos
trescientos sesenta grados, asoman
y exploran en balde, dónde ambas manos
ocultan el otro puente que les nace
entre veras y litúrgicas bromas.

Vuelve la frontera a probar
las dos piedras que no alcanzan a ocupar
una misma posada a un mismo tiempo.
La frontera, la ambulante batuta, que sigue
inmutable, igual, sólo
más ella a cada esguince en alto.

Veis lo que es sin poder ser negado,
veis lo que tenemos que aguantar,
mal que nos pese.
¡Cuánto se aceita en codos
que llegan hasta la boca!

LIII

Who cries out eleven o'clock is not twelve!
As if they'd been bid up, the hands confrot   *
two by two eleven times.

    A brutal butt. Crowns
peer out to hear,
but without violating the eternal
three hundred and sixty degrees, they peer out
and explore in vain, where both hands
hide the other bridge that conceives them
between the truth and liturgical jokes.

    Again the border tests
two stones that don't manage to occupy
the same spot at the same time.
The border, the ambulant baton, that thrusts on
immutable, the same, only
more itself with each swerve on high.

    You see what is powerless to be denied,
you see what we have to endure,
like it or not.
How much is oiled in elbows
that reach to the mouth!

LIV

Forajido tormento, entra, sal
por un mismo forado cuadrangular.
Duda. El balance punza y punza
hasta las cachas.

A veces doyme contra todas las contras,
y por ratos soy el alto más negro de las ápices
en la fatalidad de la Armonía.
Entonces las ojeras se irritan divinamente,
y solloza la sierra del alma,
se violentan oxígenos de buena voluntad,
arde cuanto no arde y hasta
el dolor dobla el pico en risa.

Pero un día no podrás entrar
ni salir, con el puñado de tierra
que te echaré a los ojos, forajido!

˙LIV

Outcast torment, enter, leave
through a single quadrangular outlet.
Doubt. Oscillation stabs and stabs
up to the hilt.

Sometimes I hit against all the againsts,
and for moments I'm the blackest height of the apexes
in the fatality of Harmony.
Then the circles under my eyes irritate divinely,
and the sierra of my soul sobs,
the oxygens of good will force their way,
what does not burn burns and even
pain doubles up in laughter.

But one day you won't be able to enter
or to leave, with the fistful of dirt
I'll fling into your eyes, outcast!

LV

Samain diría el aire es quieto y de una contenida tristeza.

*Vallejo dice hoy la Muerte está soldando cada lindero a cada
hebra de cabello perdido, desde la cubeta de un frontal, donde
hay algas, toronjiles que cantan divinos almácigos en guardia, y
versos anti sépticos sin dueño.*

*El miércoles, con uñas destronadas se abre las propias uñas
de alcanfor, e instila por polvorientos harneros, ecos, páginas
vueltas, zarros,*
zumbidos de moscas
cuando hay muerto, y pena clara esponjosa y cierta esperanza.

Un enfermo lee La Prensa, como en fasistol.
Otro está tendido palpitante, longirrostro,
cerca a estarlo sepulto.
Y yo advierto un hombro está en su sitio
todavía y casi queda listo tras de éste, el otro lado.

Ya la tarde pasó diez y seis veces por el subsue-
lo empatrullado,
y se está casi ausente
en el número de madera amarilla

LV   *

Samain would say the air is calm and of a contained
, sadness.   *

Vallejo says today Death is soldering each limit to each
strand of lost hair, from the bucket of a frontal, where there
is seaweed, lemon balm that sings of divine seedbeds on the
alert, and antiseptic verses with no master.

Wednesday, with dethroned fingernails peels back its
own nails of camphor, and instills through dusty sieves,
echoes, turned pages, exekretion,
                the buzzings of flies
when there is a corpse, and clear spongy suffering and some
hope.

A sickman reads La Prensa, as if at a lektern.   *
Another is laid out palpitating, longirostrine,
about to be buried.
And I notice a shoulder is still in place
and almost stays ready behind this one, the other side.

The afternoon has now passed sixteen times through the
empatrolled subsoil,   *
and is almost absent
in the yellow wood number

de la cama que está desocupada tanto tiempo
                    allá...
                                        enfrente.

on the bed that's been unoccupied for so long
over there...

in front.

LVI

Todos los días amanezco a ciegas
a trabajar para vivir; y tomo el desayuno,
sin probar ni gota de él, todas las mañanas.
Sin saber si he logrado, o más nunca,
algo que brinca del sabor
o es sólo corazón y que ya vuelto, lamentará
hasta dónde esto es lo menos.

El niño crecería ahito de felicidad
                    oh albas,
ante el pesar de los padres de no poder dejarnos
de arrancar de sus sueños de amor a este mundo;
ante ellos que, como Dios, de tanto amor
se comprendieron hasta creadores
y nos quisieron hasta hacernos daño.

Flecos de invisible trama,
dientes que huronean desde la neutra emoción,
                    pilares
libres de base y coronación,
en la gran boca que ha perdido el habla.

Fósforo y fósforo en la oscuridad,
lágrima y lágrima en la polvareda.

LVI

Everyday I wake blindly
to work so as to live; and I eat breakfast,
not tasting a bit of it, every morning.
Not knowing if I have achieved, or more never,
something that explodes with flavor
or is merely the heart and that returned now, will lament
how far this is the least.

A child could grow up bloated with happiness
           oh dawns,
before the grief of parents unable to allow us
to wrest this world from their dreams of love;
before those who, like God, from so much love
understood themselves even as creators
and loved us even to doing us harm.

Fringes of an invisible weft,
teeth that ferret from neuter emotion,
          pillars
free of base and crown,
in the great mouth that has lost speech.

Match after match in the blackness,
tear after tear in clouds of dust.

LVII

Craterizados los puntos más altos, los puntos
del amor, de ser mayúsculo, bebo, ayúno, ab-
sorbo heroína para la pena, para el latido
lacio y contra toda corrección.

    ¿Puedo decir que nos han traicionado? No.
¿Qué todos fueron buenos? Tampoco. Pero
allí está una buena voluntad, sin duda,
y sobre todo, el ser así.

    Y qué quien se ame mucho! Yo me busco
en mi propio designio que debió ser obra
mía, en vano: nada alcanzó a ser libre.

    Y sin embargo, quién me empuja.
A que no me atrevo a cerrar la quinta ventana.
Y el papel de amarse y persistir, junto a las
horas y a lo indebido.

    Y el éste y el aquél.

LViI

The highest points craterized, the points
of love, of capital being, I drink, I fast, I ab-
sorb heroin for the sorrow, for the languid
throb and against all correction.

Can I say that they've betrayed us? No.
That all were good? Neither. But
good will exists there, no doubt,
and above all, being so.

And so what who loves himself so! I seek myself
in my own design which was to be a work
of mine, in vain: nothing managed to be free.

And yet, who pushes me.
I bet I don't dare shut the fifth window.
And the role of loving oneself and persisting, close to the
hours and to what is undue.

And this and that.

LVIII

En la celda, en lo sólido, también
se acurrucan los rincones.

Arreglo los desnudos que se ajan,
se doblan, se harapan.

Apéome del caballo jadeante, bufando
líneas de bofetadas y de horizontes;
espumoso pie contra tres cascos.
Y le ayudo: Anda, animal!

Se tomaría menos, siempre menos, de lo
que me tocase erogar,
en la celda, en lo líquido.

El compañero de prisión comía el trigo
de las lomas, con mi propia cuchara,
cuando, a la mesa de mis padres, niño,
me quedaba dormido masticando.

Le soplo al otro:
Vuelve, sal por la otra esquina;
apura... aprisa,... apronta!

E inadvertido aduzco, planeo,
cabe camastro desvencijado, piadoso:

LVIII

In the cell, in what's solid, the
corners are huddling too.

I straighten up the nudes that're crumpling,
doubling over, stripshredding.   *

I dismount the panting horse, snorting
lines of slaps and horizons;
lathered foot against three hoofs.
And I help him along: Move, animal!

Less could be taken, always less, from what
I'm obliged to distribute,
in the cell, in what's liquid.

The prison mate used to eat wheat
from the hills, with my spoon,
when, at my parents' table, a child,
I'd fall asleep chewing.

I whisper to the other:
Come back, go out by the other corner;
hurry up... hurry... hasten!   ·

And unnoticed I adduce, I plan,
nigh the broken-down makeshift bed, pious:

No creas. Aquel médico era un hombre sano.
   Ya no reiré cuando mi madre rece
en infancia y en domingo, a las cuatro
de la madrugada, por los caminantes,
encarcelados,
enfermos
y pobres.

   En el redil de niños, ya no le asestaré
puñetazos a ninguno de ellos, quien, después,
todavía sangrando, lloraría: El otro sábado
te daré de mi fiambre, pero
no me pegues!
Ya no le diré que bueno.

   En la celda, en el gas ilimitado
hasta redondearse en la condensación,
¿quién tropieza por afuera?

Don't believe it. That doctor was a healthy man.
    I'll no longer laugh when my mother prays
in childhood and on Sunday, at four o'clock
in the morning, for travelers,
the imprisoned,
the sick
and the poor.

    In the sheepfold of children, I'll no longer aim
punches at anyone, who, afterwards,
still bleeding, might whimper: Next Saturday
I'll give you some of my lunch meat, but
don't hit me!
Now I won't tell him ok.

    In the cell, in the gas boundless
until balling in condensation,
who's stumbling outside?

LIX

La esfera terrestre del amor
que rezagóse abajo, da vuelta
y vuelta sin parar segundo,
y nosotros estamos condenados a sufrir
como un centro su girar.

Pacífico inmóvil, vidrio, preñado
de todos los posibles.
Andes frío, inhumanable, puro.
Acaso. Acaso.

Gira la esfera en el pedernal del tiempo,
y se afila,
y se afila hasta querer perderse;
gira forjando, ante los desertados flancos,
aquel punto tan espantablemente conocido,
porque él ha gestado, vuelta
y vuelta,
el corralito consabido.

Centrífuga que sí, que sí,
que Sí,
que sí, que sí, que sí, que sí: NO!
Y me retiro hasta azular, y retrayéndome
endurezco, hasta apretarme el alma!

LIX

The terrestrial sphere of love
left behind below, goes round
and round not stopping a second,
and we are condemned as a center
to suffer its spinning.

Motionless Pacific, glass, pregnant
with all resources.
Cold Andes, inhumanable, pure.
Could be. Could be.

The sphere spins on the flint of time,
and sharpens itself
so sharply it wants to disappear;
it spins forging, before deserted flanks,
that point so terrifyingly familiar,
because it has gestated, round
and round,
the celebrated playpen.

Centrifugally yes, yes,
say Yes,
yes, yes, yes, yes: NO!
And I retreat until I turn blue, and retracting myself
harden, until I clench my soul!

LX

Es de madera mi paciencia,
sorda, vejetal.

Día que has sido puro, niño, inútil,
que naciste desnudo, las leguas
de tu marcha, van corriendo sobre
tus doce extremidades, ese doblez ceñudo
que después deshiláchase
en no se sabe qué últimos pañales.

Constelado de hemisferios de grumo,
bajo eternas américas inéditas, tu gran plumaje,
te partes y me dejas, sin tu emoción ambígua,
sin tu nudo de sueños, domingo.

Y se apolilla mi paciencia,
y me vuelvo a exclamar: ¡Cuándo vendrá
el domingo bocón y mudo del sepulcro;
cuándo vendrá a cargar este sábado
de harapos, esta horrible sutura
del placer que nos engendra sin querer,
y el placer que nos DestieRRa!

LX

Of wood is my patience,
deaf, vejetal.

Day you who've been pure, a child, a good-for-nothing,
you were born naked, the leagues
of your march, keep running across
your twelve extremities, that frowning fold
which later frays
into who knows what final diapers.

Constellated of grumose hemispheres,
under eternal unknown americas, your great plumage,
you depart and leave me, without your ambiguous emotion,
without your knot of dreams, Sunday.

And my patience is eaten away,
and I turn to exclaim: When will Sunday,
big-mouthed and mute, emerge from the sepulcher;
when will it come to load up this Saturday
of rags, this horrible suture
of the pleasure that begets us accidentally,
and the pleasure that BaniSHEs us

LXI

Esta noche desciendo del caballo,
ante la puerta de la casa, donde
me despedí con el cantar del gallo.
Está cerrada y nadie responde.

El poyo en que mamá alumbró
al hermano mayor, para que ensille
lomos que había yo montado en pelo,
por rúas y por cercas, niño aldeano;
el poyo en que dejé que se amarille al sol
mi adolorida infancia.... ¿Y este duelo
que enmarca la portada?

Dios en la paz foránea,
estornuda, cual llamando también, el bruto;
husmea, golpeando el empedrado. Luego duda
relincha,
orejea a viva oreja.

Ha de velar papá rezando, y quizás
pensará se me hizo tarde.
Las hermanas, canturreando sus ilusiones
sencillas, bullosas,
en la labor para la fiesta que se acerca,
y ya no falta casi nada.

LXI   *

Tonight I get down from my horse,
before the door of the house, where
I said farewell with the cock's crowing.
It is shut and no one responds.

The stone bench on which mama enlightened
my older brother, so he could saddle
backs I had ridden bare,
through lanes, past hedges, a country boy;
the bench on which I left my heartsick childhood
yellowing in the sun.... And this mourning
that frames the portal?

God in alien peace,
the beast sneezes, as if calling too;
noses about, prodding the cobbles. Then doubts
whinnies,
his ears all ears.

Papa must be up praying, and perhaps
he will think I am late.
My sisters, humming their simple,
bubblish illusions,   *
preparing for the approaching holy day,
and now it's almost here.

Espero, espero, el corazón
un huevo en su momento, que se obstruye.

   Numerosa familia que dejamos
no ha mucho, hoy nadie en vela, y ni una cera
puso en el ara para que volviéramos.

   Llamo de nuevo, y nada.
Callamos y nos ponemos a sollozar, y el animal
relincha, relincha más todavía.

   Todos están durmiendo para siempre,
y tan de lo más bien, que por fin
mi caballo acaba fatigado por cabecear
a su vez, y entre sueños, a cada venia, dice
que está bien, que todo está muy bien.

TRILCE

I wait, I wait, my heart
an egg at its moment, that gets blocked.

Numerous family we left
not long ago, no one awake now, and not even a candle
placed on the altar so that we might return.

I call again, and nothing.
We fall silent and begin to sob, and the animal
whinnies, keeps on whinnying.

They're all sleeping forever,
and so nicely, that at last
my horse dead-tired starts nodding
in his turn, and half-asleep, with each pardon, says
it's all right, everything is quite all right.

LXII

Alfombra
Cuando vayas al cuarto que tú sabes,
entra en él, pero entorna con tiento la mampara
que tánto se entreabre,
cása bien los cerrojos, para que ya no puedan
velverse otras espaldas.

Corteza
Y cuando salgas, di que no tardarás
a llamar al canal que nos separa:
fuertemente cojido de un canto de tu suerte,
te soy inseparable,
y me arrastras de borde de tu alma.

Almohada
Y sólo cuando hayamos muerto ¡quién sabe!
Oh nó. Quién sabe!
entonces nos habremos separado.
Mas si, al cambiar el paso, me tocase a mí
la desconocida bandera, te he de esperar allá,
en la confluencia del soplo y el hueso,
como antaño,
como antaño en la esquina de los novios
ponientes de la tierra.

LXII

Carpet
Whenever you go to the room that you know,
enter it, but carefully half-close the screen
                    that so often is half-open,
Fit the bolts tight, so that other backs
                    no longer can turn.

Peeling
And when you leave, say that you'll not delay
in calling the canal that separates us:
powerfully kaught on an edge of your fate,
I am to you inseparable,
and you drag me brinkwise with your soul.

Pillow
And only when we have died—who knows!
                    Oh no. Who knows!
will we then have separated.
But if, on changing step, I am handed
the unknown flag, I will wait for you there,
at the confluence of breath and bone,
as in old times,
as in old times on the corner of the western
                    bride and groom of the earth.

Y desde allí te seguiré a lo largo
de otros mundos, y siquiera podrán
servirte mis nós musgosos y arrecidos,
para que en ellos poses las rodillas
en las siete caídas de esa cuesta infinita,
y así te duelan menos.

And from there I'll follow you along
other worlds, and even my mossy
and cold-benumbed nos will serve you,
so you may rest your knees on them
in the seven falls of that infinite slope,
and thus they will hurt you less.

LXIII

Amanece lloviendo. Bien peinada
la mañana chorrea el pelo fino.
Melancolía está amarrada;
y en mal asfaltado oxidente de muebles hindúes,
vira, se asienta apenas el destino.

Cielos de puna descorazonada
por gran amor, los cielos de platino, torbos
de imposible.

Rumia la majada y se subraya
de un relincho andino.

Me acuerdo de mí mismo. Pero bastan
las astas del viento, los timones quietos hasta
hacerse uno,
y el grillo del tedio y el jiboso codo inquebrantable.

Basta la mañana de libres crinejas
de brea preciosa, serrana,
cuando salgo y busco las once
y no son más que las doce deshoras.

TRILCE

LXIII

Day breaks raining. Combed through
morning drips fine hair.
Melancholy is lashed fast;
and on the misasphalted oxident of Hindu furniture,   *
veering, destiny hardly settles.

Skies of the puna disheartened
by great love, platinum skies, torvus
with impossibility.

The flock ruminates and is underscored
by an Andean whinny.

I remember myself. But the staves
of the wind suffice, the rudders so still
they appear one,
and the cricket of tedium and the gibbous unbreakable elbow.

The morning suffices with free plaits
of precious, sierran tar,
when I go out and look for eleven o'clock
and it is only an ill-timed twelve.

LXIV

Hitos vagarosos enamoran, desde el minuto montuoso que obstetriza y fecha los amotinados nichos de la atmósfera.

Verde está el corazón de tánto esperar; y en el canal de Panamá ¡hablo con vosotras, mitades, bases, cúspides! retoñan los peldaños, pasos que suben, pasos que baja-
n.
Y yo que pervivo,
y yo que sé plantarme.

Oh valle sin altura madre, donde todo duerme horrible mediatinta, sin ríos frescos, sin entradas de amor. Oh voces y ciudades que pasan cabalgando en un dedo tendido que señala a calva Unidad. Mientras pasan, de mucho en mucho, gañanes de gran costado sabio, detrás de las tres tardas dimensiones.

Hoy   Mañana   Ayer.

(No, hombre!)

LXIV

Wandering landmarks enamor, since the mountainous minute that midwives and dates the insurgent niches of the atmosphere.

The heart is green from so much waiting; and in the Panama Canal—I'm speaking to you, middles, bases, cusps! stairsteps sprout, steps going up, steps going dow-
n.
And I who liveforever,
and I who know to stand firm.

Oh valley without mother height, where everything sleeps a horrible halftone, without refreshing rivers, without beginnings of love. Oh voices and cities that pass galloping on a finger pointed at bald Unity. While, from much to much, farmhands of a great wise lineage pass, behind the three tardy dimensions.

Today   Tomorrow   Yesterday

(No, man!)

LXV

Madre, me voy mañana a Santiago,
a mojarme en tu bendición y en tu llanto.
Acomodando estoy mis desengaños y el rosado
de llaga de mis falsos trajines.

Me esperará tu arco de asombro,
las tonsuradas columnas de tus ansias
que se acaban la vida. Me esperará el patio,
el corredor de abajo con sus tondos y repulgos
de fiesta. Me esperará mi sillón ayo,
aquel buen quijarudo trasto de dinástico
cuero, que pára no más rezongando a las nalgas
tataranietas, de correa a correhuela.

Estoy cribando mis cariños más puros.
Estoy ejeando ¿no oyes jadear la sonda?
               ¿no oyes tascar dianas?
estoy plasmando tu fórmula de amor
para todos los huecos de este suelo.
Oh si se dispusieran los tácitos volantes
para todas las cintas más distantes,
para todas las citas más distintas.

Así, muerta inmortal. Así.
Bajo los dobles arcos de tu sangre, por donde

LXV

Mother, tomorrow I'm going to Santiago,
to dip myself in your blessing and in your tears.
I am reconciling my disillusions and the rosy
of sore in my pointless tasks.

Your arch of astonishment will await me,
the tonsured columns of your longings
that exhaust life. The patio will await me,
the downstairs corridor with its tori and festive   *
borders. My tutorial armchair will await me,
that solid bigjawed piece of dynastic
leather, forever grumbling at the great-great-grandchild
rumps, from strap to strand.

I am sifting my purest affections.
I am axling—don't you hear the plummet gasping?   *
　　　—don't you hear the reveilles champing?   *
i am molding your love formula
for all the hollows of this floor.
Oh if only tacit fliers were available
for all the most distant cinctures,
for all the most distinct citations.

So it is, immortal dead one. So it is.
Under the double arches of your blood, where

hay que pasar tan de puntillas, que hasta mi padre
para ir por allí,
humildóse hasta menos de la mitad del hombre,
hasta ser el primer pequeño que tuviste.

Así, muerta inmortal.
Entre la columnata de tus huesos
que no puede caer ni a lloros,
y a cuyo lado ni el Destino pudo entrometer
ni un solo dedo suyo.

Así, muerta inmortal.
Así.

one can only pass on tiptoes, even my father
to go through there,
humblest himself until less than half a man,   *
until being the youngest child that you had.

   So it is, immortal dead one.
In the colonnade of your bones
which not even sobs can topple,
and in whose side not even Destiny could intrude
even one of his fingers.

   So it is, immortal dead one.
So it is.

LXVI

Dobla el dos de Noviembre.

Estas sillas son buenas acojidas.
La rama del presentimiento
va, viene, sube, ondea sudorosa,
fatigada en esta sala.
Dobla triste el dos de Noviembre.

Difuntos, qué bajo cortan vuestros dientes
abolidos, repasando ciegos nervios,
sin recordar la dura fibra
que cantores obreros redondos remiendan
con cáñamo inacabable, de innumerables nudos
latientes de encrucijada.

Vosotros, difuntos, de las nítidas rodillas
puras a fuerza de entregaros,
cómo aserrais el otro corazón
con vuestras blancas coronas, ralas
de cordialidad. Sí. Vosotros, difuntos.

Dobla triste el dos de Noviembre.
Y la rama del presentimiento
se la muerde un carro que simplemente
rueda por la calle.

LXVI   *

The Second of November tolls.

These chairs are truly welkoming.
The branch of forebodings
goes, comes, rises, lifts, undulates sweaty,
wearied in this sitting room.
The Second of November tolls sad.

Souls, how low your abolished teeth
cut, scanning blind nerves,
without recalling the tough fiber
rotund singing workers are mending
with unending hemp, with innumerable knots
throbbing with crossroads.

You, souls, of the limpid knees
pure after so many surrenderings,
how you saw at the other heart
with your white crowns, sparse
in cordiality. Yes. You, souls.

The Second of November tolls sad.
And the branch of forebodings
is bitten by a wagon that simply
rolls through the street.

LXVII

Canta cerca el verano, y ambos
diversos erramos, al hombro
recodos, cedros, compases unípedos,
espatarrados en la sola recta inevitable.

Canta el verano, y en aquellas paredes
endulzadas de marzo,
lloriquea, gusanea la arácnida acuarela
de la melancolía.

Cuadro enmarcado de trisado anélido, cuadro
que faltó en ese sitio para donde
pensamos que vendría el gran espejo ausente.
Amor, éste es el cuadro que faltó.

Mas, para qué me esforzaría
por dorar pajilla para tal encantada aurícula,
si, a espaldas de astros queridos,
se consiente el vacío, a pesar de todo.

Cuánta madre quedábase adentrada
siempre, en tenaz atavío de carbón, cuando
el cuadro faltaba, y para lo que crecería
al pie de árdua quebrada de mujer.

LXVII

Summer sings near, and we both
wander diverse, shouldering
curves, cedars, uniped compasses,
straddling on the inevitable single straight line.

Summer sings, and on those sweetened
walls of March,
the arachnoid aquarelle of melancholy
        snivels, swarms.

A picture framed with cracked annelid, a picture
missing from that spot where
we thought the great absent mirror should go.
Love, this is the picture that was missing.

But, why exert myself
by gilding straws for such an enchanted auricle,
if, on the back of beloved stars,
emptiness is tolerated, despite everything.

How much mother remained inside
always, in tenacious carbon attire, when
the painting was missing, and for what could grow
at the foot of woman's arduous ravine.

Así yo me decía: Si vendrá aquel espejo
que de tan esperado, ya pasa de cristal.
Me acababa la vida ¿para qué?
Me acababa la vida, para alzarnos

sólo de espejo a espejo.

So I told myself: If that mirror ever comes
having been so awaited, now it's more than glass.
My life was running out—to what end?
My life was running out, to raise us

only from mirror to mirror.

LXVIII

Estamos a catorce de Julio.
Son las cinco de la tarde. Llueve en toda
una tercera esquina de papel secante.
Y llueve más de abajo ay para arriba.

Dos lagunas las manos avanzan
de diez en fondo,
desde un martes cenagoso que ha seis días
está en los lagrimales helado.

Se ha degollado una semana
con las más agudas caídas; hace hecho
todo lo que puede hacer miserable genial
en gran taberna sin rieles. Ahora estamos
bien, con esta lluvia que nos lava
y nos alegra y nos hace gracia suave.

Hemos a peso bruto caminado, y, de un solo
                    desafío,
blanqueó nuestra pureza de animales.
Y preguntamos por el eterno amor,
por el encuentro absoluto,
por cuanto pasa de aquí para allá.
Y respondimos desde dónde los míos no son los tuyos,
desde qué hora el bordón, al ser portado,
sustenta y no es sustentado. (Neto).

LXVIII

It is the Fourteenth of July.
Five in the evening. It's raining all over
a blotting paper third corner.
And it rains more from below ay upward.

Two lagoons the hands advance
ten abreast,
out of a swampy Tuesday that has for six days
in the lachrymals been frozen.

A week has slashed its throat
with the sharpest falls; haz done
all that it can to make miserable genial
in a big tavern without rails. Now we're ,
ok, given this rain which washes us
and cheers us up and softly pleases us.

We've walked as gross weight, and, with a single
defiance,
our purity of animals whitened.
And we ask for eternal love,
for the absolute encounter,
for what goes on from here to there.
And we responded from where mine are not yours,
from what time the staff, on being carried,
supports and is not supported. (Net.)

Y era negro, colgado en un rincón,
sin proferir ni jota, mi paletó,
a
t
o
d
a
s
t
A

And my greatcoat, it was black,
hanging in a corner, not uttering a sound,

a
t
f
u
l
m
a
s
T

*

LXIX

Qué nos buscas, oh mar, con tus volúmenes
docentes! Qué inconsolable, qué atroz
estás en la febril solana.

Con tus azadones saltas,
con tus hojas saltas,
hachando, hachando en loco sésamo,
mientras tornan llorando las olas, después
de descalcar los cuatro vientos
y todo los recuerdos, en labiados plateles
de tungsteno, contractos de colmillos
y estáticas eles quelonias.

Filosofía de alas negras que vibran
al medroso temblor de los hombros del día.

El mar, y una edición en pie,
en su única hoja el anverso
de cara al reverso.

LXIX

What in us do you seek, oh sea, with your docent
volumes! How inconsolable, how atrocious
you are in the feverish sunshine.

With your mattocks you leap,
with your leaves you leap,
hacking, hacking in a maddened sesame,
while the waves return weeping, after
uncalking the four winds
and all memories, in labiate platters
of tungsten, contracted by tusks
and static chelonian I's.

Philosophy of black wings vibrating
in the shy tremor of the shoulders of day.

The sea, and an edition standing,
in its single leaf the recto
facing the verso.

LXX

Todos sonríen del desgaire con que voyme a fondo, celular de comer bien y bien beber.

Los soles andan sin yantar? O hay quien les da granos como a pajarillos? Francamente, yo no sé de esto casi nada.

Oh piedra, almohada bienfaciente al fin. Amémonos los vivos a los vivos, que a las buenas cosas muertas será después. Cuánto tenemos que quererlas y estrecharlas, cuánto. Amemos las actualidades, que siempre no estaremos como estamos. Que interinos Barrancos no hay en los esenciales cementerios.

El porteo va en el alfar, a pico. La jornada nos da en el cogollo, con su docena de escaleras, escaladas, en horizontizante frustración de pies, por pávidas sandalias vacantes.

Y temblamos avanzar el paso, que no sabemos si damos con el péndulo, o ya lo hemos cruzado.

LXX

Everyone smiles at the nonchalance with which I sink to the bottom, cellular from eating right and drinking well.

Do suns move without purveyance? Or is there someone who offers them grain as if to little birds? Frankly, I know almost nothing about this.

Oh stone, benefacient pillow at last. Let us the living love the living, since gratefully dead things will be later. How much we must love them and hug them, how much. Let us love actualities, for we won't always be as we are. For there are no interim Barrancos in the essential cemeteries.   *

The transport depends on the clay, edgily. The journey hits us in our vegetal core, with its dozen stairways, scaled, in a horizonifying frustration of feet, by pavid vacant sandals. *

And we tremble to take another step, for we don't know if we bang into the pendulum, or have already crossed it.

LXXI

Serpea el sol en tu mano fresca,
y se derrama cauteloso en tu curiosidad.

Cállate. Nadie sabe que estás en mí,
toda entera. Cállate. No respires. Nadie
sabe mi merienda suculenta de unidad:
legión de oscuridades, amazonas de lloro.

Vanse los carros flajelados por la tarde,
y entre ellos los míos, cara atrás, a las riendas
fatales de tus dedos.
Tus manos y mis manos recíprocas se tienden
polos en guardia, practicando depresiones,
y sienes y costados.

Calla también, crepúsculo futuro,
y recójete a reir en lo íntimo, de este celo
de gallos ajisecos soberbiamente,
soberbiamente ennavajados
de cúpulas, de viudas mitades cerúleas.
Regocíjate, huérfano; bebe tu copa de agua
desde la pulpería de una esquina cualquiera.

LXXI

The sun coils in your fresh hand,
and spreads cautious in your curiosity.

Hush. No one knows that you are in me,
all of you. Hush. Don't breathe. No one
knows of my succulent snack of unity:
the legion of obscurities, the amazons of crying.

The carts leave flajellated by evening,
and among them my own, face backwards, in the fatal
reins of your fingers.
Reciprocal your hands and mine stretch forth
poles on guard, practicing depressions,
and temples and sides.

Hush too, future dusk,
and retyre to laugh in the intimate, at this rut
of purple-reddish gamecocks magisterially,
magisterially fitted out with demilune   *
spurs, with cerulean widow halves.
Rejoice, orphan; down your shot of water
from the general store on any corner.

LXXII

Lento salón en cono, te cerraron, te cerré,
aunque te quise, tú lo sabes,
y hoy de qué manos penderán tus llaves.

Desde estos muros derribamos los últimos
escasos pabellones que cantaban.
Los verdes han crecido. Veo labriegos trabajando,
los cerros llenos de triunfo.
Y el mes y medio transcurrido alcanza
para una mortaja, hasta demás.

Salón de cuatro entradas y sin una salida,
hoy que has honda murria, te hablo
por tus seis dialectos enteros.
Ya ni he de violentarte a que me seas,
de para nunca; ya no saltaremos
ningún otro portillo querido.

Julio estaba entonces de nueve. Amor
contó en sonido impar. Y la dulzura
dió para toda la mortaja, hasta demás.

LXXII

Slow conical salon, they closed you, I closed you,
although I loved you, as you know,
and from whose hands will your keys dangle today.

From these walls we tore down the last
few pavilions that sang.
The fodder is in leaf. I see peasants working,
the hills filled with triumph.
And the elapsed month and a half is enough
for a shroud, even too much.

Salon with four entrances and without an exit,
since you are deeply morose today, I speak to you
using your six entire dialects.
No longer need I force you to be for me,
fornever; no longer will we leap
any other beloved wicket.

July was then in its ninth. Love
counted in an uneven sound. And there was enough
sweetness for the whole shroud, even too much.

LXXIII

Ha triunfado otro ay. La verdad está allí.
Y quien tal actúa ¿no va a saber
amaestrar excelentes dijitigrados
para el ratón? Sí... No...?

Ha triunfado otro ay y contra nadie.
Oh exósmosis de agua químicamente pura.
Ah míos australes. Oh nuestros divinos.
    Tengo pues derecho
a estar verde y contento y peligroso, y a ser
el cincel, miedo del bloque basto y vasto;
a meter la pata y a la risa.

Absurdo, sólo tú eres puro.
Absurdo, este exceso sólo ante tí se
suda de dorado placer.

LXXIII

Another ay has triumphed. The truth is there.
And whoever acts that way, won't he know
how to train excellent dijitigrades
for the mouse? Yes... No...?

Another ay has triumphed and against no one.
Oh exosmosis of water chemically pure.
Ah my southerns. Oh our divines.
     I have the right then
to be green and happy and dangerous, and to be
the chisel, what the coarse colossal block fears;
to put my foot in and to my laughter.

Absurdity, only you are pure.
Absurdity, only facing you does this excess sweat golden pleasure.

LXXIV

Hubo un día tan rico el año pasado..!
que ya ni sé qué hacer con él.

Severas madres guías al colegio,
asedian las reflexiones, y nosotros enflechamos
la cara apenas. Para ya tarde saber
que en aquello gozna la travesura
y se rompe la sien.
Qué día el del año pasado,
que ya ni sé qué hacer con él,
rota la sien y todo.

Por esto nos separarán,
por eso y para ya no hagamos mal.
Y las reflexiones técnicas aun dicen
¿no las vas a oir?
que dentro de dos gráfilas oscuras y aparte,
por haber sido niños y también
por habernos juntado mucho en la vida,
reclusos para siempre nos irán a encerrar.

Para que te compongas.

LXXIV

One day last year was so rich....!
that now I don't know what to do with it.

Stern mother guides at school,
kept an eye on our reflections, and we hardly let   *
fly our faces. Only to later discover
the hanky-panky hinges on that   *
and breaks our temples.
What a day that was last year,
right now, I don't know what to do with it,
cracked temple and all.

For this they'll separate us,
for that and so we'll no longer act up.
And our technical reflections still say
—aren't you going to hear them?
that inside two dark and apart milled edges,
for having been children and likewise
for having gotten together so much in life;
they're going to lock us up prisoners forever.

So that you'll compose yourself.

LXXV

Estais muertos.

Qué extraña manera de estarse muertos. Quienquiera diría no lo estais. Pero, en verdad, estais muertos.

Flotais nadamente detrás de aquesa membrana que, péndula del zenit al nadir, viene y va de crepúsculo a crepúsculo, vibrando ante la sonora caja de una herida que a vosotros no os duele. Os digo, pues, que la vida está en el espejo, y que vosotros sois el original, la muerte.

Mientras la onda va, mientras la onda viene, cuán impunemente se está uno muerto. Sólo cuando las aguas se quebrantan en los bordes enfrentados, y se doblan y doblan, entonces os transfigurais y creyendo morir, percibís la sexta cuerda que ya no es vuestra.

Estais muertos, no habiendo antes vivido jamás. Quienquiera diría que, no siendo ahora, en otro tiempo fuísteis. Pero, en verdad, vosotros sois los cadáveres de una vida que nunca fué. Triste destino. El no haber sido sino muertos siempre. El ser hoja seca, sin haber sido verde jamás. Orfandad de orfandades.

LXXV   *

You're all dead.

What a strange way of being dead. Anyone would say
you aren't. But, truly, you're all dead.

You float nothingly behind that membrane that, pendu-
lating from zenith to nadir, comes and goes from dusk to
dusk, vibrating before the sonorous box of a wound that
hurts none of you. Verily, I say unto you that life   is in the
mirror, and that you are the original, death.

While the wave goes, while the wave comes, with what
impunity does one stay dead. Only when the waters crash
against facing banks, folding and doubling, do you then
transfigure yourselves and believing you are dying, perceive
the sixth string that no longer is yours.

You're all dead, not having lived before ever. Anyone
would say that, not existing now, in another time you might
have. But, verily, you are the cadavers of a life that never was.
A sad fate. The not having been but always dead. Being a
dry leaf, without ever having been green. Orphanhood of or-
phanhoods.

Y sinembargo, los muertos no son, no pueden ser cadáveres de una vida que todavía no han vivido. Ellos murieron siempre de vida.

Estais muertos.

How ever, the dead are not, cannot be cadavers of a life they have not yet lived. They always died of life.

You're all dead.

LXXVI

De la noche a la mañana voy
sacando lengua a las más mudas equis.

En nombre de esa pura
que sabía mirar hasta ser 2.

En nombre de que la fui extraño,
llave y chapa muy diferentes.

En nombre della que no tuvo voz
ni voto, cuando se dispuso
esta su suerte de hacer.

Ebullición de cuerpos, sinembargo,
aptos; ebullición que siempre
tan sólo estuvo a 99 burbujas.

¡Remates, esposados en naturaleza,
de dos días que no se juntan,
que no se alcanzan jamás!

LXXVI

All night long I keep sticking
out my tongue at the most mute Xes.

In the name of that pure one
who knew how to watch until she was 2.

In the name of that to her I was a stranger,
key and lock very different.

In the name o'her who had no voice
nor vote, when this
her fate to make was determined.

Ebullition of bodies, never the less,
apt; ebullition that always
stayed at just 99 bubbles.

Endings, married in nature,
of two days that do not come together,
that do not reach each other ever!

LXXVII

Graniza tánto, como para que yo recuerde
y acreciente las perlas
que he recogido del hocico mismo
de cada tempestad.

No se vaya a secar esta lluvia.
A menos que me fuese dado
caer ahora para ella, o que me enterrasen
mojado en el agua
que surtiera de todos los fuegos.

¿Hasta dónde me alcanzará esta lluvia?
Temo me quede con algún flanco seco;
temo que ella se vaya, sin haberme probado
en las sequías de increibles cuerdas vocales,
por las que,
para dar armonía,
hay siempre que subir ¡nunca bajar!
¿No subimos acaso para abajo?

Canta, lluvia, en la costa aun sin mar!

LXXVII

It hails so much, as if to make me recall
and increase the pearls
that I've gathered from the very snout
of every storm.

May this rain never dry.
Unless I am permitted
to fall now for it, or unless they bury me
drenched in the water
that would surge from all fires.

This rain, how far will it reach me?
I'm afraid I'm left with one flank dry;
afraid that it's ending, without having tested me
in droughts of incredible vocal cords,
by which,
to create harmony,
one must always rise—never descend!
Don't we rise in fact downward?

Sing, rain, on the coast still without a sea!

NOTES TO THE TRANSLATION

In regard to archaic, obscure, or coined words, besides many dictionaries, I have consulted the glossaries by Ferrari and Larrea, and Giovanni Meo Zilio's study of Vallejo's neologisms. Anyone who cares to compare my work with this scholarship will see that I have sometimes disagreed with these scholars. Julio Ortega feels that their work tends to be speculative and often fails to take into consideration idiomatic usage. For my part, in completing the translation and the notes, I have tried to incorporate their suggestions whenever they made any sense at all, as it is now almost impossible to determine what may have been late nineteenth century idiomatic variations in Vallejo's part of Peru. For detailed critical commentary on the poems, I refer the reader to Ortega's critical edition of *Trilce*, as well as to other books and articles in the bibliography that follows these notes. For variant readings, as well as reproductions of early versions of seven poems, I refer the reader to the Colección Archivos edition.

The earliest poems in *Trilce* were probably written before Vallejo's first book, *Los heraldos negros* (1918), was published. The only source for the dates of individual poems (the book is not organized chronologically, and Vallejo himself offers no information in this regard) is Juan Espejo Asturrizaga's biography of Vallejo's Peruvian years.

Ferrari, Larrea, and André Coyné have all disputed some of them, but in spite of some guesswork and certain questionable date-event associations, Espejo's dates are valuable. He was in close association with Vallejo during the years of *Trilce's* composition; he occasionally heard a poem read shortly after it was written, and in one case he actually watched Vallejo write a first draft. According to Espejo, forty-eight of the seventy-seven poems were written in 1919. The rest were written in the following years:

1918: LX, LXV, LXVI.

1920: XIX, XXII, XXIV, XXVIII, LII, LV, LXIII, LXVII, LXX, LXXV.

1921: VII, XIV, XXIX, XXX, XXXII, XXXVI, XLVIII.

1922: XXVI, LIX.

The remaining poems (I, II, XVIII, XX, XLI, L, LVIII, LXI) were supposedly written during Vallejo's incarceration in the Central Trujillo Jail, between November 6, 1920 and February 26, 1921. Espejo also mentions that while he was in jail, Vallejo rewrote and radically transformed poems previously written between March 1919 and April 1920. Thus it may be that the poetics of *Trilce* were worked out during his incarceration.

I have not annotated all irregular or "difficult" words. While I have commented on words I consider to be neologisms, I have not noted words in which one letter is replaced with another in such a way that only the appearance (and not the sound) is slightly changed. I have simply made a corresponding change in the English word to alter its appearance but not change its sound. For example, when Vallejo misspells *facistol* as *fasistol,* I misspell "lectern" as "lektern." If words—no matter how uncommon—may be found in the second or third edition of *Webster's New Internatio-*

nal Dictionary, I have not commented, unless I have deviated from what one might anticipate the translation to be. I have tried to stay clear of interpretations, preferring to let the reader deal with *Trilce's* complexities. For biographical tie-ins, we refer the reader to Espejo (and to Ferrari's notes in the Colección Archivos edition) —with the warning that in spite of his clearly comradely intentions, Espejo often uses fairly simple biographical information to explain poems that to varying degrees have consumed their referentiality in their writing. I have also scrupulously respected Vallejo's punctuation. Even when it is irregular (and a bit out of sync with what might be the English equivalent), it strikes me as being intrinsic to the way a phrase or line should be voiced.

Trilce was published in October 1922. The following June, Vallejo sailed from Peru for Europe. In the fall of 1923, a poem called "Trilce" appeared in the Spanish magazine *Alfar*. This poem has not turned up in the various editions of Vallejo's posthumous European poetry, and there is no way to know where he felt it belonged (indeed, in tone and form it does not clearly belong to *Trilce* or to the European poems). Larrea, who seems to have known Vallejo as well as anyone during the European years (1923–1938), but who chronically presents speculation as fact, proposes that this poem was written in Peru when the *Trilce* manuscript was complete but was still being called by an earlier title, "Cráneos de bronce" ("Bronze Skulls," probably with indigenous skin-coloring in mind). At the point which Vallejo was presumably persuaded to change the book's title, Larrea writes, the poet transferred the title of this poem to the book (without, for unexplained reasons, including the poem itself). For those, like me, who suspect the story about the spontaneous discovery of the word "trilce" (the one based on Vallejo's supposed stuttering), this is an interesting notion, as it backs up my suspicion that the word "trilce" was worked out independent of the "stuttering incident." However, Ferrari points out that there is no proof for Larrea's explanation whatsoever, and the fact that the poem was not included in the second Madrid edition of *Trilce* (1930) indicates that Vallejo did not want it to be part of the book. José Rubia Barcia and I included a version of "Trilce" in our *César Vallejo: The Complete Posthumous Poetry* (Los Angeles: Univ. of California Press, 1978). It seems appropriate to include a revised translation of the poem here.

TRILCE

There is a place that I myself know
in this world, no less,
we will never reach.

Where, even if our foot
were to reach it for an instant
it will be, truly, as if we are not there.

It is that spot which is seen
every moment in this life,
walking, walking in single file.

This side of myself and of
my pair of yolks, I have glimpsed it
always distant from destinies.

Now, you can depart on foot
or out of sheer sentiment bareback,
since not even stamps could reach it.

The tea color horizon
is dying to colonize it
for its great Whatever part.

But the place that I myself know,
in this world, no less,
sought pace with its opposites.

—Close that door that
is ajar in the entrails
of that mirror. —This one? —No; its sister.

It cannot be closed. It is not possible
to ever reach that spot
where the bolts act up unbound.

Such is the place that I myself know.

* * *

I:

Espejo writes that while Vallejo was in the Trujillo jail, inmates
were taken outside to use the latrines four times a day. Instead of
allowing the men to take their time, the guards shouted at them,

reviling them and demanding that they hurry up. This is extremely useful background information for this particular poem.

Guano, the dried excrement of seabirds, found mixed with bones and feathers on certain Peruvian coastal islands, was a widely used fertilizer. Guano workers visited the mainland ports and cities on their days off, and Vallejo would have been able to observe them not merely in Trujillo itself, but in the vicinity of the jail.

calabrina (ponk): Archaic, "an intolerable, intense stench." If it were translated simply as "stench," the translation would reflect the common Spanish word *hedor*. Thus the necessity, in such cases, of finding archaic English words (or expressions) for their Spanish equivalents.

tesórea (fecapital): Based on *tesoro* (treasure), this word has provoked differing interpretations. Meo Zilio identifies it as a neologism that incorporates the latter part of *estercórea* (excrement), influenced by the guano references in the stanza (as well as by the first stanza, which may refer to the guards shouting at the men in the latrines, creating "islands"). Ortega hears the "órea" as a beautiful, almost flowery, sound, evoking Rubén Darío.

abozaleada (muzzled): Based on *abozalada* (muzzled), substituting an *-ear* infinitive ending for the standard *-ar* ending. Meo Zilio considers the word to be a neologism; Ortega hears it as idiomatic, northern Peruvian speech.

II:

cancionan (song on): *Canción* (song) forced to function as the verb *cantar* (to sing).

Qué se llama cuanto heriza nos? (What call all that stands our end on hAIR?): *Heriza* appears to be a fusion of two verbs: *eriza* (bristles) and *hiere* (wounds). Larrea proposes that this neologism is based on *horripilar* (to horripilate, to make one's hair bristle, or stand on end). Since there is no way to fuse "bristles" and "wounds," and since the Latinate and rare "horripilate" misses the idiomatic playfulness of the Spanish, I have taken a slightly different route by playing with the notion of hair standing on end. By reversing the verb and its object, Vallejo redirects the emphasis, which my inversion attempts to pick up, as it also redirects the meaning of "end." At the same time, spotting the "air" in "hair," I lift it up, as Vallejo might have, had he seen its equivalent in Spanish. This sense of seizing words by their hair, as it were, and pulling them this way and that is endemic to *Trilce*. At the beginning of the line, the replacement of *Cómo se llama* with *Qué se llama* is regional and idiomatic.

III:

Santiago: The old, blind bell-ringer of Santiago de Chuco, Vallejo's birthplace and hometown.

Aguedita, Nativa, Miguel: Vallejo's two youngest sisters and his youngest brother.

penas (souls in torment): A Peruvianism.

IV:

trifurcas (trifurca): A neologism based on *trifurcado* (trifurcate).

amargurada (embitternessed): A neologism derived from *amargura* (bitterness) and *amargar* (to embitter).

espiritiva (spiritive): *-iva* (ive) added to *espíritu* (spirit).

qué la bamos a hhazer (what'her we gonna dooo): A sound and syntactic distortion of *qué vamos a hacer con ella* (what are we going to do about, or with, her, or it). Possibly infantile, possibly local, possibly sheer Vallejo.

dosificarse en madre (to double mother's dose): While the verb clearly means "to dose," the fact that *dos* (two) is part of it has to be taken into consideration, given Vallejo's obsessive use of primary numbers in the book. Larrea goes so far as to say that *dosificarse* here means *desdoblarse* (to unfold, split). I see the *dos* as significant, but not so significant as to take over the basic meaning of the word.

V:

avaloriados (rhinestoned): A neologism probably based on *avalorar* (to value) and *abalorio* (glass beads, or any showy article of little value).

glise: Probably based on the French *glisser* (to glide). Evocation of *glissé* (in ballet, a glissade, or glide).

VI:

otilinas (Otilian): Based on the first name of Vallejo's lover in Lima (1918–1919), Otilia Villanueva. When she became pregnant and Vallejo refused to marry her, Otilia was sent away by her family to San Mateo de Surco in the sierra, and the poet lost his position as Director of the Instituto Nacional, a private school with which Otilia's family was involved.

fratesadas (lustred): An old Spanish word meaning "to give a luster to hose after washing them," using a glass or wood trowel-shaped object.

capulí de obrería (tawny berry of handiwork): According to the 1870 *Diccionario de peruanismos* (repr., Paris: Desclée, de Brouwer; Biblioteca de cultura peruana, Vol. 10, 1938), the *capulí* (*Prunus capuli*) is a bush that yields a flower and a dark yellow berry, much appreciated throughout the Peruvian sierra for its delicate, ornamental beauty. Ferrari adds that *color capulí* is similar to *moreno* (dark-complexioned, swarthy) and *trigueño* (olive-skinned: see line 14 in the same poem). "Capulín" appears to be the English equivalent; *Websters* defines it as a Mexican tree with a *red* berry. In regard to *obrería* Vallejo's usage appears to be idiomatic and to refer solely to Otilia as an *obrera* (worker) i.e., a laundress. He implies in this line that Otilia is the fruit if her own labor.

VIII:

hifalto (saltatory): From the Greek *hyphállomai*. Rare, ornithological word for birds that walk hopping. Dr. Carlos Senar of the Zoological Museum of Barcelona, who researched the word for me, writes that "it has a taxonomic meaning and so can be used to refer to all birds of the Order Passeriformes." The largest order of birds, Passeriformes includes over 7,000 species and sub-species. Ferrari wrote to me that he understands *el hifalto poder* as "the power that moves via hops," stressing the idea of discontinuity or leaps. I disagree with several critics and translators who believe that the word is a neologism based on *hijo* (son) and *falto* (lack). "Saltatory," from the Latin *saltare*, "to leap," is defined in *Webster's Second New International Dictionary* as "proceeding or taking place by a leap or leaps, rather than by gradual, orderly, continuous steps or transitions."

IX:

Espejo offers an anecdote that he considers pertinent to this poem: Vallejo found himself in a darkened room with a masked woman who passionately offered herself to him. He had no idea who she was. The two were together for several days, and without revealing each other's identity, confided intimately in each other. Espejo also explains that according to Vallejo, the substitution of "v" for "b" in several words, as well as its repetition, graphically emphasizes "vulva." As in the case of the *heriza* problem in II, it was not possible to find a direct match for this variation, so I have attempted to register the sound and word play in a slightly different way.

todo avía verdad (all readies truth): The first two words in Spanish play off *todavía* (yet, still, nevertheless), while the second word sounds like a past tense of *haber* (to have).

enveto (I transasfixiate): *Envetarse* is a rare verb that has at least two meanings, both of which may be operative here. In Ecuador, it means "to dominate"; according to Neale-Silva, Vallejo uses it in this sense in a 1927 article, "El arco del triunfo," in speaking of *un fornido mozo en actitud de envetar un toro* (a husky youth getting ready to subdue a bull). The use of *toroso* (torose, taurine) in the third stanza supports this meaning. However, in Peru the word also means "to become asphyxiated by the poisonous emanations from the veins of a mine," and given the context of "Bolivarian asperities" (rugged landscapes in which mines might very well exist), this meaning also seems pertinent (though I notice that by using the verb actively, Vallejo reverses its passive usage as a mining term).

X:

arzonamos (we saddleframe): The noun *arzón* (saddleframe) forced to function as a verb.

y sentado empavona tranquilas misturas (and seated enpeacocks tranquil nosegays): According to the *Diccionario de peruanismos*, a *mistura* is a small bouquet of local, fragrant flowers, such as frangipani, jasmine, passion flower, gillyflower, including for additional ornamentation such berries as the *capulí*—see note on VI. In this setting, the standard meaning of *empavonar* (to blue steel, or, in Latin America, to grease) seems most inappropriate. In Central America, *empavonar* can mean the same as *emperifollarse* (to doll oneself up), a meaning that draws upon *pavón* (peacock) and *pavonear* (to strut). I interpret the line to mean that the patient is arranging nosegays in a vain way that evokes peacock display.

XII:

Tramonto (Tramontation): This word appears to be a noun-like neologism based on the verb *tramontar*, which can mean to cross the mountains, sink behind the mountains (as the sun), or, reflexively, to help someone escape. It is clearly linked to *tramontana*, in English, "tramontane" (on the other side of the mountain, or a cold, violent northerly wind). In an early version of XV (dated by Espejo in 1919), we find the word used in the last two lines: *¡Son dos puertas abriéndose, cerrándose, al huir / Sombra a sombra en mitad de este tramonto!* Here it is clear that *tramonto* is being used as a noun (probably eliminating the possibility that it could be a first person singular of the verb *tramontar*), and, given the context of doors blowing open, that Vallejo probably has the violent wind meaning in mind. However, in an early version of XII (dated 1921, and reproduced in the Colección Archivos edition), *Ocaso* (occident, or the setting of the sun) occupied the place of *Tramonto* in the second line. Given the uncertainty of any choice here, I have opted for "tramontation" (archaic according to the O.E.D.), which means the setting of the sun behind a mountain.

fabrida (factures): Old Spanish for *fabricar* (to fabricate, manufacture).

XIII:

hijar (daughterloin): By adding a silent "h" to *ijar* (loin, or flank), Vallejo strongly evokes *hija* (daughter).

XIV:

goma (rubber): Escobar (and Vega, in agreement with him) reads *azogue* (quicksilver) in this line as a metaphor for semen. Such a reading is made plausible by line 6, and stimulated by the beasts in line 4 (because of their association with the sexually-driven beast in line 12 of the preceeding XIII). I therefore translate *goma* not as "glue" but as "rubber". For another erotic use of quicksilver, see XXVII, line 12.

un sueldo de cinco soles (a wage of five soles): The sol is Peru's monetary unit. Such a wage would have been virtually nothing.

XV:

cuja (bed): A Latin-Americanism.

Daudet: Alphonse Daudet (1840–1897), a French writer, known among other books for *Lettres de mon moulin* (1869), a collection of Provence-inspired short stories. This poem was originally written as a sonnet called "Sombras" (Shadows) (see Colección Archivos edition).

XVI:

ceros a la izquierda (zeros on the left): Also an idiomatic expression meaning "mere ciphers" or "nobodies." I translate it literally here, as part of Vallejo's preoccupation with the left and with negative numbers (e.g., the book's title, and poems IV, XXV, and XXXVIII).

Cangrejos, zote! (Dunce, lice!): In Alonso's *Enciclopedia del idioma* (Madrid, 1968), *zote* (dunce) has the following additional meaning: "In dances typical of Calcarlos, *zote* is the cry shouted at the dancers when they are to leap up." The word may be related to the french *sautée*, also a dance term. Alonso also cites *cangrejo* (crab) as having, in Peru, the slang meanings of *felón* (villain, scoundrel) and *bribón* (idler, loafer, bum).

XVII:

ovulandas (ovulatable): That which can be ovulated. According to Ferrari, the word is based on the verb *ovular* (to ovulate), using "the adjectival ending of a passive Latin conjugation." The same formation is found in *callandas* (silence-deserving) in XXV.

XIX:

Jean Franco writes, in regard to the first line, "by giving Hope a Greek name (Hélpide) and capitalizing the initial letter, Vallejo is creating his own deity." However, Meo Zilio points out that Vallejo has added an "H" to the Greek *elpis, -idos*, and by doing so has evoked the *Helpis*, or *Helpido*, a genus of spiders (which elsewhere make two appearances in *Trilce*: the adjective "arachnoid" in XL and LXVII).

A trastear . . . escampas (To descant . . . you babble): Both verbs have a cluster of denotations, and in this line there is little contextual reinforcement for any particular meaning. My translation is based on line 15 ("and to speak to me you arrive chewing ice"), where there is not only a reference to speech, but to the difficulty of speech. It is possible that this line refers back to line 1, in which "descant" and "babble" are among the denotations.

XX:

chirota (gullery): An old word for mischief or trickery. There is a remote possibility that it could be a distortion of *chirote* (a kind of linnet), or that it could play off *chirona* (slang for jail, the clink).

XXI:

arteriado (arteried): A neologism based on *arteria* (artery). In LVII, Vallejo does the same thing with *crater* (crater), turning it into *craterizados* (craterized).

Hubimos de esplendor (We had to splendor): Apparently a mix of *tuvimos esplendor* (we had splendor) and *hubimos de esplender* (we had to shine). While "splendor" does exist as a verb in English, it is sufficiently rare to pick up at least some of the deft oddness of the Spanish phrase.

XXII:

Don Jacobo está en hacerio (M. Jean Jacques is in the black books): Jean Jacques Rousseau is undoubtedly referred to; *en hacerio* is an archaic phrase meaning "in utter disgrace or misfortune." Like *calabrina* in the first poem, it is appropriately rendered by a word/phrase archaic in English.

chirapa (rainshines): In northern Peruvian Spanish, "to rain while the sun is shining" (based on the Quechua *chirapani*).

XXIII:

silenciar (silency): Read by Larrea as a neologism, meaning to remain in a state of silence. It is also possible that Vallejo has simply forced the verb *silenciar* (to silence) into a noun state.

XXV:

Alfan alfiles (Thrips uprear): The common meaning for *alfil* is "chess bishop" (based on the Arabic *al-fil*, or elephant, the original form of the bishop). A much less common meaning is *agüero* (omen, augury). The verb *alfar* appears to refer to the action of a horse that raises its head too high while galloping (I have not been able to track down the context for this denotation, i.e., does it relate to dressage? Arabic horsemanship?). Meaningwise, a good case can be made for "chess bishop," since in chess the bishop is next to the knight, which is a horse head, the juxtaposition might possibly have triggered *alfan alfiles*. However, the magic of the line is in the sound connection (with the first two words followed by *a adherirse*—to adhere), so I have rejected a literal meaning-oriented translation of the line that might go: "Chess bishops hold their (horse) heads too

high to adhere . . ." Because the *alfiles* seem to function as destructive agents that attach themselves to a number of unrelated and
related things (which subsequently unravel, collapse, hobble, and
wheeze), I have decided to work with a reading of *alfiles* which I
acknowledge is questionable. I propose, with the marriage of sounds
also in mind, to read it as a variant of *alfilerillos*, which can denote a
destructive insect (a kind of flea beetle, which leaps up—or slightly
stretched, a thrip). To some extent, in a poem as multidirectional as
XXV, certain word choices become compromises relative to other
words. For example, in line 4, *cadillos* can be translated as "cockle-
burs" or as "thrums" (warp ends, which can be associated with
"unraveled" in line 5), and by selecting "thrips" for line 1, I thus get,
in line 4, "thrips and thrums"—a sound play that may be as unusual
as the sound play between the first two words in Spanish in line 1.
While my translation of *Trilce* is primarily meaning-oriented, there
are occasions when the sound play is so paramount that it must be
given equal priority with meaning (other examples: XX, line 1; XXIII,
line 1; XXIV, lines 2–3; XXX, lines 16–17). It is also important in a
poem like XXV not to select a "program" at the beginning and then
veer as many meanings as possible into its stream. In an essay on
Hart Crane in *At Their Word* (Santa Barbara: Black Sparrow, 1978),
Cid Corman perceptively writes:

> . . . typical of what we think *is* Crane would be the piled-up
> shifting metaphorical language, verbal gorgeousness outrun-
> ning sense, of:

> > (Let sphinxes from the ripe
> > Borage of death have cleared my tongue

Once and again; vermin and rod
No longer bind. Some sentient cloud
Of tears flocks through the tendoned loam:
Betrayed stones slowly speak.)

Vallejo seems incipient. And Rimbaud's love of shock of language, of mere verbality. And Thomas in his even tighter conjunctions. This impulse towards mobbing sense is of our time.

While I would tend to disagree with Corman's *critical* stance here, his association of these lines from Crane's magnificent "Lachrymae Christi" with Vallejo (in general, I gather) makes a lot of sense, especially with such poems as *Trilce* XXV in mind.

ennazala (ennasals): A neologism based on "nasal," adding a prefix and turning the adjective into a verb.

innánima (innanimous): A neologism based on *inánime* (lifeless, inanimate). This word is paired with *grifalda* (gerfalcon, or gyrfalcon), old Spanish for the falcon of that name. A gerfalcon is also a small culverin (in Spanish, a *grifalto*). This meaning also appears to be involved.

XXVI:

aurigan (are charioted by): The noun *auriga* (chariot) turned into a verb.

sinamayera: A female vendor of Philippine sinamay, a textile woven of abaca fiber.

sures: Southerly winds on the coasts of Chile and Peru.

XXVIII:

El yantar (Viandry): An archaic word that as a noun refers to food. It is also a medieval term for the tax or provisions given to a monarch by a town, as he and his entourage pass through. I emphasize this second (or perhaps initially primary) meaning in LXX: *Los soles andan sin yantar?* (Do suns move without purveyance?), since in this case the sun in its daily course seems to be compared to a monarch in pilgrimage. As a verb, *yantar* used to be a common word meaning "to eat." While it would be out of common usage for most Spanish speakers today, it may still be in use in remote sierra areas of Peru.

XXX:

vagoroso (vagurant): A neologism fusing *vago* (vague) and *vagaroso* (vagrant).

XXXI:

entre algodones (cotton coddled): Literally, "between cottons, or cotton pads/wads." The phrase appears, however, to make us of the expression *estar criado entre algodones* (to be kept or wrapped in cotton-wool, i.e., to be coddled, or pampered).

XXXII:

Rumbbb. . . . . . Trrraprrr rrach . . . . . . chaz (Rooombbb. . . . . . Hulllablll llust . . . . . . ster): While these sounds may be read as street noise, the fact that the words *trapa*, *racha*, and *cachaza* (which appears as such in line 9) seem to be involved, invites me to reconstruct the line making use of English equivalents. With poetry, the challenge is always to translate everything.

NOTES TO THE TRANSLATION

Serpentínica u del bizcochero (Serpenteenic e of the sweet roll vendor): The "u" of the *bizcochero*'s cry—"*biscochouus*"—unwinds in the air like a serpentin (a roll of colored paper which is cast forth so as to unroll, as at a carnival). I change the "u" to an "e" to pick up the sound of "ee" in "serpenteenic," as well as the "ee" in "sweet" (which is echoed in line 13, along with the long "o" in "rolls" (Weeeeeetrozzz).

enjirafada (girafted): A neologism fusing *jirafa* (giraffe) and *enjertar* (a variation on *injertar*, to graft).

XXXIII:
incordes (incordant): A neologism based on *discorde* (discordant, dissonant).

XXXVI:
a las ganadas (hellbent on winning): A northern Peruvianism.

amoniácase (ammoniafies): *amoníaco* (ammoniac, ammonia) turned into a verb. While we have a verb in English (ammonify), I do not use it, as there is none in Spanish.

todaviiza (neverthelessez): The adverb *todavía* (yet, still, nevertheless—and, in old Spanish, always) extended/warped into a verb. A few lines later another adverb, *aunes* (evens), is treated as a plural noun.

XXXVII:
marinera: A gallant, coastal Peruvian folk dance.

XXXIX:

Mésome (I yank out): The verb *mesarse* is conventionally accompanied by an object e.g., *mesarse el pelo* (to tear out one's hair). Here the verb also appears to evoke *mecer* (to swing), since *a columpio* (on a swing) appears in the next line.

XL:

lunesentes (Mondayescent): A neologism that appears to juxtapose *lunes* (Monday) with the suffix *-escentes* (-escent, denoting beginning, or beginning to be). While *lunescentes* also evokes *luna* (moon, from which Monday derives), given the stanza's context of "Sunday" and "six elbows" (the other days of the week?), Monday appears to be the neologism's primary significance.

XLI:

tas / con / tas (slap / for / swap): A *tas* is a small anvil used by silversmiths, called a "stake" in English. Given the context of beating/striking (and the evocation of jail masturbation in the first stanza), this meaning of *tas* appears to be involved. However, *taz a taz* (tit for tat) and *taz con taz* (even, equal, as in a score tied 7 to 7), are perhaps equally strong candidates for the phrase upon which Vallejo's variation is based. And since we know that he often slightly deforms words, changing visual appearance with the sound more or less intact, it is possible that *tas con tas* is a visual alteration of *taz con taz*. While it is always possible in such a situation to pick the most likely meaning and translate it literally, it is more adventuresome (and more in keeping with the maverick spirit of *Trilce*) to create a phrase in English that while involving the implications of the original is as unusual as Vallejo's variation.

XLVI:

An earlier version of this poem (a sonnet called "La Tarde"—The Evening—reproduced in the Colección Archivos edition) contains Otilia's name. Espejo recalls: "One evening, when all of us were wandering around the city [Lima], we found ourselves overlooking the Balta Bridge. It was getting dark, and at the end of the bridge we paused, taking in the tree-lined Cantagayo Avenue, where on her table a woman streetvendor was displaying anticuchos, Huancaina-style potatoes, cau-cau, glasses brimming with corn chicha, and gorgeous ears of corn. César had been here once with Otilia. He was profoundly moved, and against a ledge of the bridge, on the back of a racing-form, he wrote 'La Tarde.'" For a reference to a racing-form, see XXXV.

XLVII:

te desislas (you deisland): *Isla* (island) turned into a "negative" verb by the addition of the prefix *des-* (de-). Possibly based on such standard verbs in Spanish as *desterrar* (to banish, or exile; literally to de/earth), and *desaislarse* (to come out of seclusion or isolation; literally to de/isolate). The sense here is that the archipelago disintegrates into the depths of the sea.

pericotes (mice): A Peruvianism.

XLIX:

iridice (irisizes): A neologism fusing *iride* (the stinking iris, or gladdon) with *iridiscente* (iridescent) into a verb.

causas (mashed causes): *Causas* are causes in English, too, but *la causa* is a purée of boiled potatoes mashed with oil and lemon. Given the food associations in the last three lines of this poem, I feel that the compound phrase in English is appropriate.

L:

el corvino (This raven): Ortega believes that *corvino* here is the masculine for *corvina*, a common Peruvian fish (known in English, too, as corvina, and related to the weakfish or grouper) used in such dishes as ceviche. He bases his opinion on another conjecture, that in the second stanza *mojarilla* also refers to a fish (the *mojarra*, the same in English). In Peru, he comments, street-smart boys are sometimes referred to as *corvinos* or *mojarillas*. The other possibilities: all dictionaries offer "crow-like, corvine" as definitions of *corvino*, and I suspect that the Cerberian warden in the poem is more crow-like than fish-like, and that he may evoke for the jailed Vallejo Poe's raven, as a figure of "nevermore." Also, all dictionaries list *mojarilla* as meaning "a gay, or jolly person," with no mention of the fish (it being listed solely as *mojarra*). Since we have just been told (in line 8) that the warden "jokes with the prisoners," it is possible that Vallejo intends to deepen his cynicism in the following line by referring to him as "jolly." Given the lack of definite evidence for either position, I have gone with the reading that the poem itself seems to back up most cogently.

LIII:

se afrotan (the hands confrot): Since I believe that the subject of the verb is the hours, specifically the hours as indicated by the hands of a clock, I add "hands," so that the subject (otherwise, simply "they") will not be confused with the subject of *Quién clama* (Who cries out) in the first line. *Se afrotan* appears to be a neologism based on *afrontar* (to confront) and *frotar* (to rub or to frot).

LV:

Espejo, who was hospitalized in the summer of 1920, writes that this poem was composed in response to hospital visits made by Vallejo.

Samain diría (Samain would say): Vallejo quotes from the first two lines of "L'automne," by Albert Samain (1856–1900), which, translated by Juan Ramón Jiménez, was included in *La poesía francesa moderna* (1913), edited by Diez-Canedo and Fortun. This is the book that introduced Vallejo to French Symbolist poetry. Among the poets included were Nerval, Baudelaire, Gautier, Corbière, Laforgue, Rimbaud, Verlaine, Mallarmé, Jammes, Maeterlinck, and Claudel. Samain's poetry, written in a Symbolist vein, was distinguished by its melancholy tone and musical qualities. Franco calls the quoted poem "a nostalgic evocation of human alienation healed by the essential harmony of nature." *Trilce* explicitly demonstrates a rupture with this kind of Symbolism. Here is the original of the Samain poem:

> Comme dans un préau d'hospice ou de prison,
> L'air est calme et d'une tristesse contenue;
> Et chaque feuille d'or tombe, l'heure venue,
> Ainsi qu'un souvenir, lente, sur le gazon.

Le Silence entre nous marche . . . Coeurs de mensonge.
Chacun, las du voyage, et mûr pour d'autres songes,
Rêve égoïstement de retourner au port.

Mais les bois ont, ce soir, tant de mélancolie,
Que notre Coeur s'émeut à son tour et s'oublie
A parler du passé, soûs le ciel qui s'endort,

Doucement, a mi-voix, comme d'un enfant mort.

At one point Espejo dates LV in 1919, but after mentioning his hospitalization in 1920, he dates the poem in that year. It occurs to me that after 105 days in jail, Vallejo would have been extremely sensitive to a description of the air in a prison yard as "calm," especially if he associated this place with being shouted at while using outdoor latrines (see my commentary on the first poem in *Trilce*). Thus a case might be made for LV having been composed in 1921, after Vallejo's release from jail.

La Prensa: One of the principal daily newspapers of Lima.

empatrullado (empatrolled): A neologism based on *patrullado* (patrolled).

LVIII:

se harapan (stripshredding): A neologism based on *harapo* (rag) and probably *arroparse* (to clothe oneself, wrap up). Since the *desnudos* (nudes) in the line above are probably pin-ups the prisoners have tacked to the wall, I attempt to create a word that inverts *arroparse* so as to evoke "stripping" by turning one's clothes into rags.

LXI:

Espejo writes that this poem responds to a journey back to Santiago de Chuco made by Vallejo and some friends after the poet had been away for several years. He recalls: "We made an arduous journey on mule back from Menocucho [the nearest train connection to Trujillo at the time]. César's brother, Miguel, was with us. We arrived after a three-day ride, entering the town at two in the morning. Everyone was sleeping peacefully, in a delicious silence. At the Vallejo house, we knocked on the door, with César anxious to embrace his family. We knocked and knocked, and still no one responded. After a long wait, we went inside."

bullosas (bubblish): A neologism, possibly based on *bullir* (to boil, bubble) and/or *bullicioso* (bustling, boisterous).

LXIII:

oxidente (oxident): A neologism fusing *occidente* (Occident) and *oxidar* (to oxidize).

LXV:

tondos (tori): Round moldings (torus, in the singular), not to be confused with Shinto temple gateways!

ejando (axling): *Eje* (axle) turned into a verb.

tascar dianas (reveilles champing): This mysterious phrase might also be translated as "dianas scutching" or "bulls-eyes crunching." It appears, however, to play off *tocar diana* (to sound reveille), which would eliminate the other two denotations of "diana." *Tascar* means to scrutch or swingle flax, as well as to nibble, browse, or champ (as in "to champ against the bit"). Perhaps the impassioned sensation here is that of trumpet blasts trying to break the constraints of reveille and reach the dead mother. To awake the dead.

humildóse (humblest): According to Meo Zilio (and to Antenor Orrego before him), Vallejo has taken an archaic verb, *humildarse*, and substituted it for the current *humillarse*. Meo Zilio quotes Orrego: "When he says *humildarse* instead of *humillarse*, reviving an archaism in the language, the habitual semantic cap has been broken and the word has been transformed, now signifying tenderness and loving reverence. The father does not lower and humiliate himself before his wife [see stanza 4], he exalts his love and gives it a tender reverence *humbling himself* until less than half a man, / until being the youngest child that you had.'" I am not aware of such a distinction in English, though the difference between to humble and to humiliate may be close (the former implying self-abasement without the loss of respect; the latter always implying ingnominy). The translation problem is that to render *humildóse* as "humble," does not, as such, sound a difference with "humiliate."

LXVI:

Neale-Silva suggests that behind this poem commemorating All Souls Day are the deaths of Vallejo's first sweetheart in Trujillo, María Rosa Sandoval (10 February, 1918), and his mother, María de los Santos Gurrionero (8 August, 1918). Since he unconventionally capitalizes "Noviembre" and "Julio" (in LXVIII), I capitalize the full dates, as in Fourth of July, etc.

LXVIII:

The horizontal part of the last stanza looks like a flag flying from the pole made by the vertical formation *atodastA*, a compression of *a toda asta* (based on the expression *a media asta*, at half mast).

LXX:

Barrancos: Barranco is a Lima beach resort (now part of the city) that Vallejo used to frequent.

horizontizante (horizonifying): *Horizonte* (horizon) fused with *izante* (as in *electrizante*, electrifying). Note that in Spanish, the *izon* and *izant* sounds in *horizonizante* play against *escaleras* an *escaladas* in the same sentence.

LXXI:

ennavajados / de cúpulas (fitted out with demilune / spurs): *Ennavajados* is a neologism based on *navaja* (razor), to which a prefix and past participle suffix have been added. Larrea comments that the phrase refers to the attaching of demilune razors to the spurs of the gamecocks. Literally, "enrazored with cupolas."

LXXIV:

enflechamos (we . . . let fly): A neologism based on *flecha* (arrow) and *enflechado* (loaded, with arrow ready—said of a bow).

gozna la travesura (the hanky-panky hinges): *Gozna* is a neologism, based on *gozne* (hinge) and *engoznar* (to hinge). By dropping the prefix, Vallejo evokes *gozar* (to enjoy oneself, even in a sexual way), suggesting that the *travesura* (mischief) involved sexual games. Unable to pick up this aspect of the phrase in the verb, I attempt to suggest it in my choice of noun.

LXXV:

Espejo writes that "on the 27th of April [1920], we left the port of Callao, on the steamer *Aysen*, for Salaverry, arriving on the 30th. At this time, Vallejo had with him in a binder most of the poems that would make up 'Trilce.' His friends met us at the Trujillo station. Having just arrived from Lima, where he had been embroiled in quarrels and agitation, and in a constant flurry of activity, Vallejo was floored by the placid ambience, and immediately seemed to lose once and for all his interest in Trujillo. At the same time, he discovered his old friends asleep on their feet, going through life as if in 'slow motion.' The following day he brought to my house, and read, the poem beginning 'You're all dead.'" As Ferrari points out, the poem clearly transcends such an incident—yet at the same time, it is interesting to know its setting. In *César Vallejo: The Dialectics of Poetry and Silence*, Jean Franco quotes a convincing paragraph by the painter Macedonio de la Torre on the early twentieth century tedium of Trujillo.

C.E.

Vallejo's Succulent Snack of Unity

Clayton Eshleman

One of the most striking portraits of César Vallejo comes from the Peruvian novelist Ciro Alegría who was one of Vallejo's students when the young poet worked as a grade-school teacher in Trujillo in 1915. Alegría was only six years old when he first laid eyes on Vallejo.

César Vallejo—I've always thought that was the first time I saw him——had his hands on the table and his face turned toward the door. Below his abundant black hair, his features showed deep and definite lines. His nose was energetic and his chin, more energetic still, jutted out like a keel. His dark eyes——I don't recall if they were grey or black——shown as if there were tears in them. His suit was old and rumpled, and his white shirt collar was closed by a carelessly-looped little tie. He began to smoke, continuing to look toward the door through which came the bright light of April. He was thinking or dreaming who knows what. From his whole being flowed a great sadness. Never have I seen a man who appeared more sad. His grief was at once secret and visible, and after a while it infected me. A certain strange and inexplicable pain went through me. Though he seemed at peace, there was something deeply ripped apart in this man that I could not understand, but that I felt with the quick, alert sensitivity of a child. Suddenly, I found myself thinking about my birthplace, the mountains I had crossed, the life I had left behind. Studying my teacher's face a little more, I decided that he resembled Cayetano Oruna, a peasant on our hacienda, who was called Cayo. Cayo was taller and more robust, but their faces, both with an expression that was between solemnity and sadness, were very similar. This man Vallejo struck me as a message from the earth. I kept watching him. He put out his cigarette, pressed his forehead, ran his fingers through his dark hair and returned to his thoughts. His lips twisted into a painful contraction. Cayo again. But Vallejo's personality was disquieting even just to see. I was very perturbed by then and began to suspect that, from so much suffering and from literally radiating sadness, Vallejo had to have something to do with the mystery of poetry. He turned slightly, looked at me, and we looked at each other. The other students were reading their books, so I opened mine. I couldn't see the words and wanted to cry . . .[1]

Young Alegría must think back to a sierra peasant to connect with his mysterious teacher because Vallejo is from the sierra, and in demeanor and manner different from the coastal Peruvian. Vallejo's indigenous situation is complexed by the fact that both of his grandfathers were Jesuit priests from Galicia, Spain, and both of his grandmothers were Chimú Indians. Under his revolutionary warping of the Spanish language, one feels a *cholo* (a person of mixed Spanish and Indian blood) struggling not only with his identity but with a resentment against the Spanish language itself, a colonial imposition on an indigenous people. In his first book, *Los heraldos negros* (1918), Vallejo, in fairly conventional verse, had made a number of gestures toward Inca terms and themes. Such gestures disappear in *Trilce* (to my knowledge there is only one Quechua word in the book—see note on poem XXII), while at the same time Vallejo's indigenous personality becomes manifest through the atmosphere of sadness, solemnity, and austerity in the poems themselves. The last line of the last poem—"Sing, rain, on the coast still without a sea!"—appears to refer to the Peruvian sierra, where there is indeed no sea, but where the awesome mountain ranges may feel "coastal" relative to the Peruvian lowlands, desert, and jungle—areas with considerably differing cultures.

* * *

Trilce's title is a neologism and the gate guardian of the book. This masterpiece of international modernism has its perilous, heroic predicament embedded in its title, and sewn, via the title, like filaments, into the work itself.

The story goes that Vallejo had originally called the book "Cráneos de bronce" (Bronze Skulls), and had planned to sign it with the pseudonym "César Perú" (perhaps in the spirit of Anatole France). At the last minute, friends convinced him that the pseudonym was a mistake; however, the first pages had already been printed, and the author was told that the cost to reprint them would come to *tres libras*, a small amount, but money he really didn't have. His friend Juan Espejo Asturrizaga recalls: "Vallejo repeated 'tres, tres, tres,' several times, with that insistence he had for repeating and deforming words, 'tresss, trisss, triesss, tril, trilssss.' He got tongue-tied, and in the process 'trilsssce' came out . . . 'trilce? trilce?' He paused for a moment and then exclaimed: 'O.K., it will carry my own name, but the book itself will be called *Trilce*.'"

Other commentators have conjectured that the word was formed by fusing *triste* (sad) and *dulce* (sweet). While there is no reason to believe that Espejo made this story up, I believe that the poems contain internal evidence that attests to the neologism's conceptual status, which is involved with the meaning of the book at large and goes considerably beyond an impulsive deformation of words. In his memoir of Vallejo's Peruvian years, Espejo constantly offers anecdotes and recollections as explanations for the meanings of poems that remain utterly enigmatic in spite of his commentary. His anecdote explaining the origin of the word "trilce" is in the same spirit.

A more thoughtful response to the formation of the word was made by Henry Gifford who, with Charles Tomlinson, translated a dozen or so poems from *Trilce* in the early 1970s. Gifford writes: "For 'trilce,' Vallejo compounded two numerals, *trillon* and *trece*, a trillion and thirteen. A truncated trillion is held prisoner by the ill-chanced and broken thirteen. Or, perhaps, like the arm of the Venus de Milo in another *Trilce* poem, it should be seen rather as uncreated, subject to the 'perennial imperfection' of life."

Gifford does not support his numerical observation with evidence from *Trilce*, but the evidence is there. In an early version of

XXXII which appeared in a Lima newspaper in 1921, the last line read:

¡Tres trillones y trece calorías! . . .

It is possible that at some stage of revising/completing the book, Vallejo spotted the potentially new word in this line, and, pulling the *tril* from the left side of *trillones*, and the *ce* from the right side of *trece*, coined "trilce." And while the *tri-* and the *tre-* of the two key words signify "three," it is fascinating to notice what happens to that three, and to the zeros, when *lones* and *tre* are shed: *tril* signifies a one, followed by an ambiguous number of zeros (since before it can complete the eighteen zeros found in the Spanish *trillon*—which in American English means "quintillion," not "trillion"—it is truncated and hooked onto *ce*). And by eliminating the *tre* from *trece*, Vallejo has made use of only the latter part of the word, which signifies ten (like the English "teen" in "thirteen"). Thus written out as a number, "trilce" looks something like this:

1,0000000000000000... 10

While it *evokes* threeness, there is no actual three in it. Instead, we have a ghost of threeness, and a mass of indefinite zeros, with the one of trillion bounding the left, and the one of ten nearly bounding the right—a word, in effect, that is without interior determination.

So, how might we textualize "trilce"? In XVI, we find that the poet seeks to "galloon [himself] with zeros on the left."[2] Since the greatest part of the zero mass is on the "tril" (left) side of "trilce," such a line suggests that Vallejo may have been aware of the title idea—if he had not already coined the word itself—when XVI was written. (Espejo claims that the poem was written in 1919.)

In XXXVIII, we are informed that a mysterious crystal "has passed from animal, / and now goes off to form lefts, / the new Minuses." Again, "the new Minuses," especially of or on the "left," could very well refer to the nebulous zero mass of "trilce."

The word "left" first appears in the book at the end of the very cryptic poem IV: "Heat. Ovary. Almost transparency. / All has been cried out. Has been completely veiled / in deep left." While *en plena izquierda* can be translated in a number of ways (in full left, in the heart of left, right in the left, at the height of left, etc.), contextual considerations back up this translation of the phrase. This is not a high nor a full left, but a deep one, with an indefinite extension that is negative, of the underworld, as opposed to positive, of height or heaven.

At the end of XXXVI—Vallejo's *ars poetica*—readers are commanded to "Make way for the new odd number / potent with orphanhood!" Surely this new odd number is "trilce" itself, word and title, Vallejo's own Via Negativa, with orphanhood (suggested by the ones) stranded in a milky way of zeros, or, to turn the meaning slightly, "trilce" as an orphan potent because self-conceived, and belonging to the world of poetry, not to the world of numbers that we use to block out time.

* * *

Once potency and orphanhood are associated with "trilce," we find ourselves in the thick of the book, immersed in Vallejo's complex

relation to his two power sources, his mother and Otilia Villanueva. Much of the burden of *Trilce* is the transformation of a mother-
son, via a lover, into an orphan-poet who has foetal and phallic
status at the same time. To think of two orphan ones in a milky
way of zeros can be to sense the speaker in the mother of the left
and, at the same time, in the lover of the right, charging the title
with the strife of the book itself.

The major psychological pressure in *Trilce* is the vise of sex and
death. Through certain eating scenes, entangled with elegaic mother sensations and acute erotic registrations, the tomb/womb space
of the mother is explored as the body of a lover is caressed and, by
implication, consumed. In its deep structure, *Trilce* achieves its
freedom-in-tension by incestuously breaching the wall that divides
masculine energy between being a son and being a lover. When
such a wall breaks, a new, terrible heaven and hell pervade con-
sciousness.

To be a self-created orphan is quite an accomplishment, but to
be an orphan, regardless of how one became orphaned, is a severe
limitation: one is dependent, with no protection or advantage, and
in this sense one is certainly not free. *Trilce's* uniqueness is shaped
by a sense of self-isolation, as if to attain such uniqueness it had to
cut itself off from the·precursor support-system of the Latin American and (by way of translation, in Vallejo's case) French Symbolist
poetry of the past. The book seems at once *deprived* and *new,*
emaciated and *fresh.* Words such as "potent" and "orphanhood" jar
in a way that evokes André Breton's term, "exploding/fixed," for
the Surreal image.[3]

Vallejo's nostalgic portrayal of his mother juxtaposed with his severe, shapely treatment of the ruins of his experience remind me of certain paintings by Arshile Gorky—in particular the early "The Artist and His Mother" set next to the late "The Liver is the Cock's Comb." In Gorky's life, fifteen years separate these two paintings, and one feels the slow, dreadful advance into the self that the journey between the two represents. Another aspect of *Trilce*'s uniqueness is that, written in a period of less than four years, it juxtaposes thematic narratives—the poetic equivalent of the early Gorky painting—with dense, empty-and-lush lyrics, whose multiple directions are compatible, writing-wise, with Gorky's late canvasses. While it would be going too far to say that *Trilce* contains multiple personalities, the stylistic differences (scrambled throughout the book so as to appear without pattern) are so great that the reader may feel, in passing from poem III to IV, for example, that he has turned the page of Robert Lowell's "Skunk Hour" to find Charles Olson's "La Préface."

In XIX, Vallejo speaks of the necessity of burning all bridges. *Trilce* is filled not only with burned bridges, but with intact ones, or one might say: with models of what is being burned. The most striking writing in the book is involved with fracturing the referential functions of communicative language in a way that anticipates projective verse and language poetry by a number of decades. Some of the book's potent orphanhood, then, consists of a two-way movement between the inside and the outside. There are interiors, in which the act of writing generates associative clusters released from temporal and spacial obligations, and exteriors which, via sketches of childhood, romance, and jail confinement, establish a documented life. The exteriors create frames in which an interior freedom is discovered and contested (unlike Artaud, Vallejo does not make a shambles of the reality principle—his transgressional crossings are always discreet). And while poems III and IV offer a real sense of the book's oppositional poetics, such friction more often than not exists as fibers or circuits that tangle within individual poems, or even stanzas. *Trilce* may be the first twentieth-century poetic text to propose an intensely gregarious and autistic doubling that sets forth a coherent picture of the creative personality.

* * *

In *Trilce*, the only free being is "the free beast / who takes pleasure where he wants, where he can" (XIII). While the speaker envies "the beast" his supposed ability to express sexual desire spontaneously, he also understands that as a man he is neither sexually nor imaginatively free. On an imaginative plane this is so because Vallejo believes that too much of his life—which in XXXIII is said to extend back via the womb into infinite Vedic time—had passed before he became conscious that he had a life at all. It had passed, it will not return, and it cannot be redeemed. For Vallejo, the hour of birth is also the darkening of the light. In XLVII, he tells us that for the infant groping in his crib for something to take hold of, it is "already one o'clock."

To believe this is to give mother and early childhood an enormous size (thus the vast zero depth of the left side of the "trilce" formation). It follows that without imagination, life is a predetermined depression unto death. Even with an extraordinary effort of imagination (imagining, as Vallejo does, that he has yet to be born), only a truce, or holding-pattern, can be attained. Under these circumstances, the artist is tempted to sell himself the notion that through poetry itself one can be free. Such a view is solidly renounced in LVII. Vallejo calls his suspect freedom "Harmony," with its attendant henchman, perfection. Much of his *ars poetica* (XXXVI) is involved with fighting for coherence while marshalling an argument against being taken in by an idealization of our relentlessly imperfect, odd-numbered, state.

* * *

We must now look at some of the numbers which bounce, spill, and roll, sometimes alone, sometimes in clusters, through *Trilce*'s seventy-seven poems.

Four evokes confinement and constraint. When it is located in the company of three, it ceases to be simply negative and becomes formal boundary, or, to borrow William Blake's term, "the circumference of energy." In poem IV, we find "The whole song / squared by three silences." Tercet silences evoke the Trinity, but since Vallejo felt that the Trinity had been emptied of significance, Father, Son, and Holy Ghost are depicted as three zeros. I have mentioned how threeness is enghosted in the word "trilce" itself. If the book has a single, diaphanous waver, it is in the way that it nods toward a childlike yearning for the spiritual significance of the Trinity, and also nods away, toward us, to question the veracity of all traditional systems.

A more packed, and negative, use of three/four appears in poem X. It may be useful to quote this short passage, to invite the reader

to confront Vallejo's thoughtful obliqueness rather than pass over
it as poetic effect:

> How whales cut doves to fit.
> How these in turn leave their beak
> cubed as a third wing.
> How we saddleframe, facing monotonous croups.

One way to read this might be the following: the doves, or
meek ones, tailored on the basis of the whales' notion of size, continue to tailor themselves on their own (the poor man becomes his
own policeman and does not break the shop window to get bread
for his starving family); they treat their beaks as merely another aspect of their anatomy, not an outlet for protest, let alone song and
poetry.

In *Trilce*, the move from three to four—"cubed as a third
wing"—is always a retreat. The result of this mistaken and con-
strictive process is to mistake the saddle for oneself, to turn oneself
into a seat for others. To do so is to face the ass not only of the
rider, but of the viewpoint to which one has allowed oneself to be
magnetized. In reading this stanza, it is crucial to notice that Vallejo has turned *arzón* (saddleframe) into a verb. If one does not notice this, one may read it as "to saddle up" (as other translators
have), which will ruin an appropriate reading of "facing monotonous croups."

While there are occasional hints of alchemical lore, I think the
basic sense of number in the book originates in response to physical
experience which is set against the extent to which life is numeri-

cally framed and hexed. Vallejo was the youngest of eleven children. His mother was forty-two when he was born. As the youngest of the eleven, he seems to have been acutely aware of the burden of the four youngest children on his—by Peruvian sierra standards—aging mother. The four youngest find themselves abandoned as a little group at dusk in poem III, and in XXIII—the first of a set of poems to receive the weight of the mother burden to be transformed—the same four are seen as gaping baby bird beaks waiting to be fed. They are then immediately reidentified as his mother's "beggars." In the fourth stanza, Vallejo finds himself nearly paralyzed by the thought of swallowing the last morsel of food fed to him by his mother, who has been identified at the beginning of the poem as his "radiant bakery" as well as the "yolk" of his "sweet rolls." She is thus responsible for his form as well as for his content. Nourishment is fundamental to the ontology of *Trilce*, but before saying more about it, a few other things should be mentioned in regard to number.

The oppressive sense of four is reinforced by the 105-day incarceration at the end of 1920. XVIII is nominated by "the four walls of the cell." In XXII, the speaker is pursued by "four magistrates," presumably the tribunal of judges who wanted to return Vallejo to prison.

Two is more ambiguous than three or four. It is the sign of repetition and fruitless duality, and of mother and son, lover and lover. Doubleness seems to have several possibilities in *Trilce*: it can stale and repeat itself (XV), press into trinity (V), or multiply out evenly to become "the thirty-two cables" of IX or "the three-hundred and sixty degrees"—a clock face around which two hands continually end up facing each other at frozen attention—in LIII.

AFTERWORD

Aside from the title itself, the feminine space of zero is first sounded in V, where it "wakes the I and makes it stand." And the roman numeral V itself would have indicated femininity to Vallejo, as he makes erotic use of the letter "v" in IX.

Three is the most mobile and playful of *Trilce*'s numbers: it appears as the yonic triangle (XI), triples to become the nine months of gestation (X), appears as a three-year-old girl (XX), expands to "999 calories" (XXXII), and becomes the yin/yang symbol—69—of the transformational coin in XLVIII.

However, three is always shadowed by the spectral threeness of the book's title, a massive deflation of Catholic confidence. The prayer world of both parents is just that: hope without presence. But Vallejo is still touched by this world. Given his surgical mind, I find it moving that he acknowledges nostalgia and even sentimentality as still-active childhood habitations. When certain Christian figures appear, they are usually decapitalized like the "two marys" of XXIV that dethrone Mary into a secular company, which by implication can occur again and again throughout time. The lover in LXII offers his "mossy and cold-benumbed nos" as knee rests for the other—not Jesus—"on the seven falls of that infinite slope." The suggestion that ordinary people reenact Christ's Stations of the Cross, and the prayer to "saintgabriel" to "impregnate the soul" (XIX), look forward to the poems that Vallejo will write years later in Paris, where life, rimmed with dying, is at once sacred and secular.

* * *

Reflecting on a long, rich life in 1983, Kenneth Burke commented, after criticizing D. W. Winnicott's psychoanalytic model for turning the child into a "Momma's boy": "I didn't think from what I read of Winnicott that he brought out the necessary *making* of a *division*. For instance, to me this is the great beauty of Baudelaire's poem, 'La Geante,' that poem of crawling over a woman as a giantess, like a mountain. The genius of the poem is in its way of confusing the distinction between maternal woman and erotic woman."[4]

Burke seems to be praising Baudelaire, at least in the poem, for refusing to make the distinction. On an unconscious dream level, we never leave our mothers. We are pulled from the maternal womb into that of the firmament (Blake's "Mundane Shell"), and in that sense we wander wombwise tombward as long as we wander/breathe at all.[5] There is something revolting about this to Western man; against cyclical return (death, the first pact life makes with itself), he has posed the fantasy of personal immortality, devastatingly tied to sexism and its amplification, war.

Some of the ambivalence toward freedom in *Trilce* is an ambivalence toward the mother's size (and, in contrast, toward the lover's lesser stature—if the mother is associated with the zero depth of the left side of "trilce," the right side, with its diminutive ten, belongs to the lover). Shadowed by outer mother dark, Vallejo fails to achieve a reciprocal relationship with any of the several lovers who move in and out of *Trilce's* image of "the other." The lover is viewed as a figure involved with constructing a marriage trap, with the implication that to be married and, even worse, to become a father, is to be finished as an imagination. When the lover is not viewed as a pathetic seducer, she appears as an anonymous sexual engine. Such evasions of courtship as one finds in XXXIV, XXXVII, and XLVI, make for the flattest reading in the book. On the other hand, the pieces driven by a death-anxious, sexual mesh (IX, XXX, XLIII, and LXXI, for example) are keen and plangent.

The most dramatic poems in *Trilce* deal with mother as source (XXIII), mother as absence (XXVIII), lover as mother substitute (XXXV), family—mother included—as asleep forever (LXI), and mother as the immortal dead one (LXV). This group, flanked by the two groups mentioned above, creates the deep structure of the book; these are the tectonic plates on which the entire surface sits and shifts. The five poems concerning the mother operate as a cycle: leaving the source, having adventures away from it, and returning to it, burdened and somewhat enlightened. XXXV has one quite revealing stanza, and since it falls at the far point of Vallejo's circular arc away from and toward mother, it is worth looking at now:

> Lunch with her who might be
> serving the dish that we liked yesterday
> and is repeated today,
> but with a bit more mustard;
> the absorbed fork, her coquettish radiance
> of a pistil in May, and her modesty
> worth two cents, to quarrel about a straw.
> And the lyric and nervous beer
> watched over by her two nipples without hops,
> of which you shouldn't drink so much!

The third or fourth time I read this stanza I blinked, suddenly grasping its last three lines, hearing the phrase "nursing a beer" in an entirely new way! Literally, he is drinking a beer facing her across a table, aware of her breasts. But the lines really say that he is drinking from her nipples, and once that is noticed, one glances back up the stanza noticing that the eating imagery is a playful, if devious, veneer of the couple's sexual relationship. To call this oral copulation does not go far enough; the speaker portrays himself as both a nursing infant and a sexual adult. Against these lines I want to set a stanza from XXVIII. The story here, told by Espejo, is that the poet had been eating from time to time with the Espejo family. One day when Vallejo was coming to lunch, the family had to eat early and leave, so Vallejo arrived to find the table with his lunch on it, but no one there to eat with. Vallejo's response:

> How could I have had lunch. How served myself
> these things from such distant plates,
> when my own hearth has surely broken up,
> when not even mother appears at my lips.
> How could I have had a nothing lunch.

Several insights can be drawn from the juxtaposition of these stanzas: eating and drinking with the lover is the bridge by which the nourishing mother is maintained as a psychic source of energy. Because drinking with the lover is experienced as an upper dis-placement of coitus, Vallejo's foetal life is recontacted. Partially being in lover is relived as totally being in mother. Again the two ones, afloat in the multiple zeros of "trilce," come to the fore, the larger mother mass to the left, the much smaller lover unit to the right.

While Vallejo's stance in these poems is one of self-empowerment, his energy bristles with the forbidden. He is involved in the dangerous game of defending against what he is also attempting to induct. Such attraction/repulsion is signaled, at the simplest level, by the continual mentionings of coming and going, entering and leaving, or opening and closing.

As long as Vallejo can behave as a son himself, the divisive Oedipal wall will remain breached, and the flow of transformational imagery will continue. Much of the book's uniqueness and obscurity, occurs through Vallejo's shifts to maintain access to psychic incest while defending against his awareness of doing so. Certain poems—XXV is a wonderful example—are thus very coherent *and* very obscure. The flow is contingent upon sonship. At the point when the son must face becoming a father, turning lover into mother and being replaced by an infant (the marriage contract, in effect), depth recedes, and the poetry risks becoming flatly social, exchanging its paradise for reportage governed by memory and linear event.

* * *

It should now be clear that the word "trilce" does indeed contain a trinity. There is not only the ghost of the Trinity, but new players in the three roles: Mother, Lover, and foetal / phallic Vallejo. In this vision of himself, he is the orphan who renders odd and potent the number that without him would be all zeros.

When Vallejo was born his father was fifty-two. In contrast to his wife, the father hardly appears in *Trilce*. But two of his four brief appearances are remarkable. In XXVIII, he is referred to as asking "for his postponed / image, between the greater clasps of sound." I think there is a birth image neatly semi-concealed in these lines: rather than praying (which he actually did before every meal), he is seen by Vallejo as asking to be delivered, his birth having been postponed by his poet son. The father's last appearance takes place in the great elegy for Vallejo's mother (LXV). The mother in death is seen as a living pantheon, whose "arches" are so holy that only the most humble can enter her. "Even my father," he writes, "to go through there, / humblest himself until less than half a man, / until being the youngest child that you had." The tone coaxes the reader to take these lines in a sentimental way, but what is actually happening is hardly sentimental: Vallejo, the youngest child, is replacing himself with his father, which on one level gets rid of his father once and for all, and on another level fulfills his desire to enter his mother. Incest as the image turbine of elegy! The material worked through in LXV gives the poet a green light to finish the book, and the family, as such, never again appears.

Trilce's resolution is made possible not only by the tunnelwork constructed by breaching the incest prohibition, but through the development and resolution of a number of other thought-units which appear and reappear fugally throughout the poems. In the first ten poems, a kind of combined-object of problems to be taken up occurs. It includes 1) the poet's discovery while in jail that much of one's life is spent facing one's own ass, 2) the collapse of the pre-

Darwinian world, 3) the struggle to avoid repeating dead initiations, 4) the contingency of male upon female, 5) the marriage trap, 6) the intersection of the sacred and the secular, and 7) the family romance. I merely mention here what could be thought of as *Trilce*'s "bundle of burden" because the reader is entitled to the difficulty and pleasure of engaging what Vallejo does with it. Some moves peter out, while others develop and become substantial in the book.

One example: the discovery in the opening poem that life is involved with sifting shit, or negation, for possible bits of gold, is immediately focused by the speaker, raising up "from behind, muzziled, unterrified / on the fatal balance line." The first attempt to revise this predicament occurs in VIII, where Vallejo proposes to run through (as if with a sword) his own front, so as to be "left with the front toward my back." That is, instead of literally turning away from one's backside (since in a sense one cannot), why not sublimate it into a more cogent form? What now has become a motif recurs in X, "facing monotonous croups," and again in XIV, "those buttocks seated upward." In these instances, Vallejo does not appear to know how to offer the problem more imaginative value, but he keeps it present, an ikon to ponder. Then, in XL, the "shadow" suddenly rears up "completely frontal," suggesting that front and back have ceased to be in opposition. They fuse in LXIX: the sea is envisioned as "an edition standing, / in its single leaf the recto / facing the verso."

Once the mother is accorded dead *and* immortal status in poem LXV, it is as if *Trilce* breathes a joyous sigh of relief, quickens its pace, and through a series of chromatic balancings—contradictions no longer felt as such—moves briskly toward LXXVII, the final poem, in which hail, rain, fire, coast, and sierra become the keys to a simultaneous descent/ascent, the powers of poetry. On our way to LXXVII, we pass the recto facing the verso, stone as "benefacient pillow," everyone smiling at César Vallejo as he urges the living to love the living, and his lover's voice informing him that every bit of him (foetally too?) is inside her. Their hands become reciprocal, and intercourse turns into a flurry of brilliantly-colored gamecocks. It is time for this orphan, who has now justified his earlier claims of potency, to rejoice over his shot not of whiskey but of water. The amount of sweetness present is too much even for a shroud. As another "ay" triumphs, only absurdity is found to be pure, and, facing the absurd, in a gesture that recalls the alchemical *rubedo*, the poet's "excess" (transmuted guano from the opening poem?) begins to "sweat golden pleasure." Suddenly all childhood discipline is envisioned as having taken place to enable Vallejo to "compose" himself. As that isolated line falls at the end of LXXIV, the having to compose himself as a schoolchild becomes the permission to have composed himself as a book. The poet who rejoiced as an orphan now states the essence of orphanhood: being dead without ever having been alive. I read this as a farewell to the totality of his background. The quite Blakean conversion of opposites into countraries with which *Trilce* ends offers a severe developmental contour to the book and releases it into itself without flattening its complexity into a single, idealized perspective.[6]

*   *   *

My comments on *Trilce* should not be taken as definitive or summational; rather, they are what I have been able to dig out of the text while translating it. I have attempted to set before the reader the extent to which the book's title appears to invade and permeate the poems, and how, in turn, its poles of mother and lover generate much of the emotional circuitry through which, around which, against which the orphan self in the poems steers his way. I have intentionally avoided discussing the book in terms of current critical jargon which, if cogent at all, only seems relevant once the book is understood on its own terms as much as is possible. My desire here, then, has been to give the reader some railings, and foot holds, but not in any way to reduce the arduousness of the climb. I have read hundreds of pages of criticism of *Trilce* in Spanish, and have used it mainly for linguistic cues. I have resisted making use of often quite speculative interpretation as a guide in actual translating. What remains to be done now, in English as well as other languages, is an evaluation of *Trilce* (and the rest of Vallejo's poetry) in a context that includes such poets as Lezama Lima, Borges, Girondo, Moro, Huidobro, and Neruda. While the most striking features of *Trilce* are of Vallejo's own making (one early commentator states that in *Trilce* Vallejo invented "surrealism" before Surrealism), it is also clear that the book was not conceived in a total void. In this sense, a study of Vallejo's borrowings from certain French Symbolists—in particular Rimbaud and Mallarmé—and from the early twentieth century avant-garde would help us understand how, before leaving Peru, he was responding to the beginnings of international modernism. Ultimately, Vallejo's poetry must be viewed within the sphere of twentieth-century world poetry, a millennial retrospective that would set him alongside Rilke, Eliot, Mayakofsky, Apollinaire, Holan, etc. To do so, I feel, would indicate even further the range of *Trilce*'s trajectory from a poetry unique for its time to a poetry that in certain aspects is still a bit beyond what English-speaking readers can understand and assimilate today.

Clayton Eshleman

1991

NOTES TO AFTERWORD

1. Alegría's commentary on Vallejo is partially reprinted in the Colección Archivos edition of Vallejo's poetry; the full text can be found in *Cuadernos americanos* 3, No. 6 (November–December 1944): 175–191.

2. See the note on this line for an alternate reading.

3. Vallejo was of course unaware of Surrealism when writing *Trilce* (the first Surrealist Manifesto was published in Paris in 1924). While in Europe, he mainly showed contempt for Surrealism, viewing it as a literary game tied in with decadent Western capitalistic society—see César Vallejo, *Autopsy On Surrealism*, Tr. by Richard Schaaf (Willimantic, Ct.: Curbstone Press, 1982). Susan Sontag's remarks on Artaud's incompatibility with Surrealist theory are applicable to Vallejo: "The Surrealists are connoisseurs of joy, freedom, pleasure. Artaud is a connoisseur of despair and moral struggle. While the Surrealists explicitly refused to accord art an autonomous value, they perceived no conflict between moral longings and aesthetic ones, and in that sense Artaud is quite right in saying their program is 'aesthetic'—merely aesthetic, he means." *Antonin Artaud: Selected Writings*, Tr. by Helen Weaver (New York: Farrar, Straus and Giroux, 1976), p. xxviii.

4. *All Area* 2 (Spring 1983): 30.

5. See the chapter "Nature," in N. O. Brown's *Love's Body* (New York: Random House, 1966) for a trenchant meditation on the extent to which we never leave the mother. Brown writes: "All walking, or wandering, is from mother, to mother, in mother; it gets us nowhere. Movement is in space; and space, as Plato says in the *Timaeus*, is a receptacle, a vessel; a matrix; as it were the mother or nurse, of all becoming. Space is a sphere or spheres containing us; ambient and embracing; the world-mothering air as atmosphere."

6. When I had basically completed the translation of *Trilce*, at the end of March 1991, I had the following dream: a black-haired woman in charge of a kitchen gives us a food package. She says: just don't learn how it was killed. I can see through the translucent wrapping a large crab gripping the breast of a chicken that appears to still be alive. Both are immersed in liquid. My companion and I take it to our place, which is under gang siege, difficult to get into——one has to enter a building surrounded by hostile addicts and thieves. We get the package into the building and to our kitchen and study it. The chicken seems to be passing an egg through her body, as if giving her life to bear this egg, which is red and glows, as the crab flexes, with its claws sunk into the chicken's breast. I fear the egg is all blood, or has no containing wall. My companion receives the egg and treats it like a treasure. We both watch the huge chicken, out on the kitchen floor now, pulsing in an agonized way, as if she wants the egg back! The crab is gone. Only the chicken (size of a large turkey), cavernous, dilated, opening and closing, trying to draw something back inside that is gone forever . . .

CÉSAR VALLEJO: A CHRONOLOGY

1892

César Abraham Vallejo is born in Santiago de Chuco, a small town in northern Peru, in a modest house at 96 Columbus Street (which is now César Vallejo Street). Though there is some dispute over the date of his birth, it was probably March 16. His parents were Francisco de Paula Vallejo Benites (1840–1924), son of José Rufo Vallejo, a Galician priest, and María de los Santos Gurrionero (1850–1918), daughter of another Galician priest, Joaquín de Mendoza. Vallejo was the youngest member of a family of eleven children, four girls and seven boys. The family led an austere life, marked by the hardships typical of the Andean region. During his early childhood the young Vallejo developed the strong religious feelings and the strong attachment to his home that his work would later reflect.

1905

After finishing elementary school in Santiago de Chuco, Vallejo is sent to boarding school at the Colegio Nacional de San Nicolás in Huamachuco. On his way there he visits the mines of Quiruvilca, which will resurface in his novel *El tungsteno* (*Tungsten*) as "Quivilca." He spends his vacations at home.

1907–1908

For economic reasons, he is enrolled as an "external student" in his third year of secondary school, and remains in Santiago de Chuco. Then, during his fourth and last year of secondary school, he begins writing his first poems.

1910

Vallejo enrolls in the School of Letters at the Universidad de la Libertad in the city of Trujillo. For financial reasons, he is soon obliged to return to Santiago de Chuco.

1911

He goes to Lima to study at the School of Sciences of the Universidad Nacional Mayor de San Marcos. Very soon thereafter he is forced to abandon his studies, again for lack of money. From May to December he tutors the children of a wealthy landowner at an estate in Acobamba. In Lima, a magazine called *Variedades* (*Varieties*) publishes a stanza of one of Vallejo's sonnets, with a sarcastic commentary.

1912

Vallejo is employed as a bookkeeper's assistant on a sugar plantation called "Rome," in the Chicama valley. Salary: 70 soles, plus food and lodging. He gets to know the plantation workers and local peasants.

1913

After resigning from his job, he enrolls in the School of Letters at the Universidad de La Libertad in March. He begins to work at the Central Boys' School No. 241, teaching botany and anatomy. As a learning device for his students, he writes explanations of scientific phenomena in verse, which are then published in the school newspaper. He reads Taine's *Philosophy of the 19th Century*, which will have a significant impact on his university thesis. He spends his vacations in Santiago de Chuco.

1914

Vallejo's second year as a student at the Faculty of Letters. He continues to teach at the Central Boys' School. In local newspapers he publishes several of the poems which, revised and with different titles, will later be included in·his first published book, *Los Heraldos Negros* (*The Black Heralds*): "Sauce," (Willow) "Hojas de ébano," (The leaves of the ebony tree) and "Terceto autóctono," (Autochthonous tercet). He reads his poetry aloud at various parties and public events.

1915

Vallejo is a third-year student at the School of Philosophy and Letters and, simultaneously, a first-year student at the School of Law. He teaches first grade at the Colegio Nacional de San Juan, and among his pupils is the future novelist Ciro Alegría. He leads a bohemian life with a group of Trujillo friends, among whom are Antenor Orrego, Alcides Spelucín, Haya de la Torre and José Eulogio Garrido, who have a decisive influence on Vallejo's intellectual formation during those years. He reads Whitman, Verlaine, Maeterlinck, Chocano, Darío, Herrera y Reissig, Kierkegaard and many others. On August 22 his brother Miguel, his favorite childhood playmate, dies. A month later Vallejo hands in his thesis, Romanticism in Spanish Poetry, fulfilling the requirements for his bachelor's degree. He publishes "Campanas muertas" (Dead bells) in *La Reforma*.

1916

Second year of legal studies. He continues teaching at the Colegio Nacional. In Lima, the magazine *Balnearios* (*Spas*) publishes his poem "Aldeana" (Village girl), which is later reprinted in magazines in Bogotá and Guayaquil. "Noche en el campo" (Night in the country) and "Fiestas aldeanas" (Village fiestas) which, under different titles, will be included in his first book, also appear in *Balnearios*. He falls in love with María Rosa Sandóval. On a trip home to Santiago de Chuco, he writes "Los arrieros" (The mule drivers) during a long wait in the Menocucho station. He begins using the pseudonym "Korriskosso," derived from one of Eça de Queiroz's characters.

1917

Third year of legal studies. He is still teaching at the Colegio Nacional, and has begun reading Spanish avant-garde magazines such as *Cervantes*. At a party, he recites the poem "Los heraldos negros." Eguren praises his verses in Lima. *La Industria* publishes an attack on Vallejo, and his friends defend him. He falls in love with Zoila Rosa Cuadra, the "Mirtho" to whom he alludes in various poems. July 16: He attends a conference on "The Drago Doctrine" where he becomes acquainted with progressive ideas on the relations between Latin American countries and foreign powers. Clemente

Palma publishes further jeering remarks on Vallejo's work in *Variedades*. During this period, Vallejo reads Ortega y Gasset, Unamuno, Azorín, Spengler, Ibsen, Tolstoi, and D'Ánnunzio. December 25: Because of problems in his love affair with "Mirtho," Vallejo attempts suicide. Two days later he leaves Trujillo for Lima where he arrives on December 30.

1918

He enrolls in the School of Letters at the Universidad de San Marcos, Lima. He meets Mariátegui and contributes to his magazine *Nuestra Época* (*Our Times*). María Rosa Sandóval dies. Vallejo finds work teaching in a private school run by the Barrós family. August 8: His mother dies in Santiago de Chuco and Vallejo plunges into a deep depression. He falls in love with Otilia Villanueva. He delivers the manuscript of *Los heraldos negros* to the printer. The director of the school where Vallejo teaches, Pedro M. Barrós, dies, and Vallejo replaces him.

1919

Vallejo is dismissed from his position at the Barrós school (which, today, is the National Institute) through the intervention of Otilia's family. His relationship with her ends. He begins teaching in the Colegio de Guadalupe. *Los Heraldos Negros* comes out toward the middle of the year, though the publication date printed in the book is 1918. It is praised in local newspapers and magazines. Vallejo begins writing the poems that will make up *Trilce*.

1920

Vallejo is suspended from his position at the Colegio de Guadalu-pe for budgetary reasons. April 27: He travels to Trujillo and visits his family in Santiago de Chuco. August 1: He finds himself em-broiled in several serious public disorders in Santiago de Chuco, which he is accused of having caused. After he is formally charged as the intellectual instigator of the events, he travels to Trujillo in-cognito and hides out in the house of some friends for several months. On November 7 he is arrested and sent to the Trujillo Central Jail. Students and intellectuals protest his imprisonment. While in prison he writes several of the poems that will be includ-ed in *Trilce* and several short narratives; he also wins a prize in a poetry contest.

1921

Through the efforts of his friends and various intellectuals, Vallejo is released from jail on parole after 112 days of imprisonment, a traumatic experience that will be reflected in his work for the rest of his life. He returns to Lima where he works at the Colegio Gua-dalupe. One of his short narratives, "Más allá de la vida y la muer-te" (Beyond life and death), wins a prize. He continues writing the poems that will form *Trilce*. In *La Crónica* he publishes a poem that contains early versions of several poems later published in *Trilce*.

1922

Trilce is published, with a prologue by Antenor Orrego. In a letter to Orrego, Vallejo writes, "The book has fallen into a total void."

266

1923

Vallejo publishes *Escalas melografiadas* (*Melographed scales*), a collection of short narratives, and *Fabla salvaje* (*Savage talk*), a short novel. He is suspended from his teaching position, and there are rumors that judicial proceedings against him may be reopened. June 17: He leaves Peru for Europe, arriving in Paris on July 13. He begins sending regular contributions to the Trujillo daily paper *El Norte*. He also contributes articles to publications in Paris and Spain, while facing severe economic hardship. His friendship with Alfonso de Silva begins.

1924

In Santiago de Chuco, Vallejo's father dies. Vallejo is still desperately seeking work in Paris. He barely manages to survive on money sent from Peru, which always takes a very long time to arrive. He writes to Pablo Abril asking for help, and applies for a grant from Spain. He meets Huidobro, Larrea, Juan Gris. He becomes seriously ill and is hospitalized for a time. The Peruvian government tries to persuade him to return to Peru. He writes several of the so-called "prose poems" and the novel *Hacia el reino de los Sciris* (*Toward the kingdom of the Sciris*).

1925

He finds employment as a secretary at the "Bureau des Grands Journeaux Latino-Américains." He begins contributing to the weekly paper *Mundial*, and will continue to do so until 1930. In June and July he falls ill once more. He travels to Madrid to collect his grant, returning to Paris in December.

1926

At the beginning of the year, his health fails once more. He meets Henriette Maisse and lives with her. The first issue of *Favorables-Parts-Poema* appears, a publication edited by Vallejo and Larrea in Paris, with articles by Huidobro, Reverdy, G. Diego, T. Tzara and Juan Gris. In it, Vallejo publishes three critical essays that are important for what they reveal about his intellectual evolution: "Estado de la literatura española" (The State of Spanish Literature), "Poesía nueva" (New Poetry), and "Se prohíbe hablar al piloto" (Do Not Speak to the Pilot). Amauta reprints the last two articles, along with the poem "Me estoy riendo" (I am laughing). He spends a short time in Spain. In Paris he meets Georgette Philippart.

1927

Vallejo contributes to the magazine *Repertorio Americano* (*American Repertory*), published in San José, Costa Rica. He gives up his grant, and lives with Henriette again temporarily. At this point, Vallejo undergoes a profound moral and intellectual crisis. He begins to take an all-consuming interest in Marxism. *Mundial* publishes "Lomo de las sagradas escrituras" (Spine of the scriptures) and the first version of "Altura y pelos" (Height and hair).

1928

With money that was supposed to have been spent on a return ticket to Peru, Vallejo travels to the U.S.S.R. for the first time, passing through Berlin and Budapest. On his return, he begins living with Georgette. In collaboration with other Peruvian writers and politicians, he composes a thesis on "the course of action to develop in Peru" and presents it to the Peruvian Communist Party which has just been founded by Mariátegui. He offers to found a Party cell in Paris. He continues to write the notes that will be collected as *Contra el secreto profesional* (*Against Professional Secrets*).

1929
In July, he goes to England, and in September, accompanied by Georgette, he sets out on his second trip to the U.S.S.R., passing through Berlin, Warsaw, Prague, Cologne, Vienna, Budapest, Venice, Florence, Rome, Pisa and the Côte d'Azure during the journey. He works on the "book of thoughts" that will be entitled *El arte y la revolución* (*Art and Revolution*).

1930
He publishes an account of his trip to the U.S.S.R. in *Bolívar*, a magazine edited by Pablo Abril in Madrid. He and Georgette go to Spain, where he meets Salinas, Alberti, Corpus Barga and others. In Madrid, the second edition of *Trilce*, with Bergamín's prologue, is published. Vallejo begins writing plays, some of them in French. He is under surveillance by the Paris police because of the political activities for which he has several times been arrested. In December, he is expelled from France and goes to Madrid with Georgette.

1931
Vallejo lives in Madrid. His novel *El tungsteno* and his travel book *Rusia en 1931: Reflexiones al pie del Kremlin* (*Russia in 1931: Reflections at the foot of the Kremlin*) are both published in Madrid. He becomes a militant member of the Spanish Communist Party and

engages in intense activism in support of the Spanish left. During this period, he forms an extremely close friendship with García Lorca. He writes the short narrative "Paco Yunque." In October he takes a third trip to Moscow for the International Writers' Congress. Back in Spain, he begins writing *Rusia ante el Segundo Plan Quinquenal* (*Russia Faces the Second Five-Year Plan*) which the publishers reject. He writes several of the poems that will be published after his death under the title *Poemas Humanos* (*Human Poems*).

1932
In February, Vallejo returns to Paris, and succeeds in obtaining permission to remain in France. He finishes *Rusia ante el Segundo Plan Quinquenal* (which will be published for the first time in 1965).

1933
His economic situation deteriorates and he and Georgette live in a series of increasingly modest hotels. The Parisian weekly *Germinal* publishes a description of Peruvian politics by Vallejo.

1934
He carries on his political activism in Paris and begins writing the political farce *Colacho Hermanos* (*Colacho Brothers*). On October 11 he and Georgette marry.

1935
In addition to his intensive revolutionary activities, he writes two screenplays and several short narratives. All of his attempts to publish the poems he has written in the past several years fail.

CHRONOLOGY

1936

The outbreak of the Spanish Civil War brings on Vallejo's most feverish and impassioned period of political militancy: he helps form the "Comités de Defensa de la República de España," attends meetings and gatherings of solidarity, writes articles in defense of the Republican cause, etc. In December he leaves for Barcelona and Madrid on a mission of information and propaganda. He is back in Paris by December 31.

1937

Vallejo is the Peruvian delegate to the "Second International Congress of Writers for the Defense of Culture" in Spain. Back in Paris he is elected Secretary of the Peruvian section of the International Association of Writers. He writes articles and descriptive accounts of the war in Spain. He founds the newsletter *Nuestra España* (*Our Spain*). He writes the play *La piedra cansada* (*The tired foot*), as well as "España, aparta de mi este cáliz" (Spain, take this cup from me) and the last of the *Poemas Humanos*.

1938

He begins campaigning to reestablish civil liberties in Peru. On March 24 he is admitted to the Clinique Générale in a state of complete physical prostration. His condition worsens and after several days of delirium he dies on Friday, April 15 at 9:20 a.m. He is buried in the Montrouge cemetery. In 1970 his remains are transferred to the Montparnasse cemetery.

1939

In January, the Republican soldiers of the Army of the East publish the first edition of "España, aparta de mí este cáliz." In July, *Poemas Humanas* is published in Paris as a posthumous homage.

A *TRILCE* BIBLIOGRAPHY

I. PRINCIPAL EDITIONS OF *TRILCE*

1922   Lima: Talleres Tipográficos de la Penitenciaría. With Prologue by Antenor Orrego.
1930   Madrid: Compañía Ibero–Americana de Publicaciones. With Prologue by José Bergamín and poem by Gerardo Diego.
1968   In *Obra poética completa.* Lima: Moncloa Editores.
1973   New York: Grossman. Bilingual edition with English translation by David Smith.
1978   In *Poesía completa.* Barcelona: Barral. Edited by Juan Larrea, with introduction and glossary.
1988   In *Obra poética.* Nanterre: Colección Archivos. Critical edition by Américo Ferrari, with introduction and notes by Américo Ferrari, critical essays, a glossary, and a bibliography.
1991   Madrid: Cátedra. Critical edition, including critical history of each poem, by Julio Ortega.

II. On *Trilce*

Abril, Xavier. *César Vallejo o la teoría poética.* Madrid: Taurus, 1963.

Ángeles Caballero, César. *Los peruanismos en César Vallejo.* Lima: N.p. 1958.

Coyné, André. *César Vallejo.* Buenos Aires: Nueva Visión, 1968.

Debicki, Andrew: "César Vallejo's Speaker and the Poetic Transformation of Commonplace Themes." *Kentucky Romance Quarterly* 17 (1990): 247–258.

Escobar, Alberto. *Cómo leer a Vallejo.* Lima: Villanueva, 1973.

Espejo Asturrizaga, Juan. *César Vallejo, Itinerario del hombre.* Lima: Mejía Baca, 1965.

Ferrari, Américo. *El universo poético de César Vallejo.* Caracas: Monte Ávila, 1972.

Flores, Ángel, ed. *Aproximaciones a César Vallejo.* 2 vols. New York: Las Américas, 1971.

Franco, Jean. *César Vallejo. The Dialectics of Poetry and Silence.* Cambridge: Cambridge University Press, 1976.

Higgins, James. *The Poet in Peru.* Liverpool: University of Liverpool Press, 1982.

_____. *César Vallejo en su poesía.* Lima: Seglusa, 1989.

Iberico, Mariano. *En el mundo de Trilce.* Lima: Universidad de San Marcos, 1963.

Larrea, Juan. "*Trilce,* cifra de aniversarios." *Ínsula* (Madrid) 332–333 (July–Aug. 1974).

_____. *Al amor de Vallejo.* Valencia: Pre-Textos, 1989.

Ly, Nadine. "*Trilce* XII. Essai d' analyse textuelle." *Les Langues Neo-Latines* 250–251 (1984): 93–102.

_____. "La poética de César Vallejo: Arsenal de trabajo." *Cuadernos Hispanoamericanos* 456–457 (June–July 1988): 641–715.

McDuffie, Keith. "*Trilce* I y la función de la palabra poética de César Vallejo," *Revista Iberoamericana* 71 (1970): 191–204.

Meo Zilio, Giovanni. "Neologismos en la poesía de César Vallejo." *Lavori della sezione fiorentina del grupo spanistico* I (1967): 5-8.

Monguió, Luis. *César Vallejo. Vida y obra.* Lima: Perú Nuevo, 1960.

Neale–Silva, Eduardo. *César Vallejo en su fase trílcica.* Madison: University of Wisconsin Press, 1975.

Ortega, Julio. *Figuración de la persona.* Barcelona: Edhasa, 1971.

_____. *La teoría poética de Vallejo.* Providence: Del Sol, 1986.

Oviedo, José Manuel. "*Trilce* II: clausura y apertura." In *Escrito al margen.* Bogotá: Pro-Cultura, 1982.

Paoli, Roberto. *Mapas anatómicos de César Vallejo.* Florence: Casa Editrice d' Anna, 1981.

_____. "Las palabras de Vallejo." In *Estudios sobre literatura peruana.* Florence: Parenti, 1985.

Pascual Buxó, José. *César Vallejo: crítica y contracrítica.* México: Universidad Nacional Autónoma de México, 1982.

Sucre, Guillermo. "Vallejo: inocencia y utopía." In *La máscara, la transparencia.* Caracas: Monte Ávila, 1975.

Vallejo, César. *Epistolario general.* Prologue and chronology by José Manuel Castañón. Valencia: Pre-Textos, 1982.

Vallejo, Georgette. *Vallejo: Allá ellos, allá ellos, allá ellos!* Lima: Editorial Zalvac, 1978.

Vega, José Luis. *César Vallejo en Trilce.* San Juan: Universidad de Puerto Rico, 1979.

Vega García, Irene. *Trilce, estructura de un nuevo lenguaje.* Lima: Universidad Católica, 1982.

Von Buelow, Christiane. "Vallejo's Venus de Milo and the Ruins of Language." *PMLA* 104 (1989): 41-52.

Wing, George. "Trilce I: A Second Look." *Revista Hispánica Moderna* 3 (1969): 268–284.

Yurkievich, Saúl, "César Vallejo y su percepción del tiempo discontinuo." In *Fundadores de la nueva poesía latinoamericana.* Barcelona: Seix Barral, 1978.

Zubizarreta, Armando. "La cárcel en la poesía de César Vallejo." *Sphinx* (Lima) (1960).